THE MARSHALL CAVENDISH
★ ★ ☆ ILLUSTRATED ★ ★ ☆

ENCYCLOPEDIA OF

WORLD WAR II

VOLUME 1

THE MARSHALL CAVENDISH
☆ ☆ ☆ ILLUSTRATED ☆ ☆ ☆
ENCYCLOPEDIA OF
WORLD WAR II

Based on the original text by
Lieutenant Colonel Eddy Bauer

CONSULTANT EDITOR

Brigadier General James L. Collins, Jr., U.S.A.

CHIEF OF MILITARY HISTORY,
DEPARTMENT OF THE ARMY

MARSHALL CAVENDISH CORPORATION/NEW YORK

CONTENTS

Editorial Director: Brian Innes
Editor-in-chief; Brigadier Peter Young, D.S.O., M.C., M.A.
Managing Editor: Richard Humble
Editor: Christopher Chant
Art Editor: Jim Bridge

FOREWORD

By Brigadier General James L. Collins, Jr., USA
CHIEF OF MILITARY HISTORY,
DEPARTMENT OF THE ARMY

1945 marked the end of the most devastating war known to mankind. In the decades since, it has faded in the memory of the participants and become a cloudy myth to many of the younger generation. It deserves better understanding, for World War II has touched the lives of all those living today and will continue to do so for the next few generations at least. It is not unique in this respect, for other major wars in our past have affected our laws, our society and even our very existence as a nation. As well as opening the nuclear age, World War II made a major contribution to American military tradition at its best. It was a war fought for a cause that was well understood and our participation was precipitated as the immediate result of a sudden, damaging blow to our forces. How our Armed Services rallied from their wounds, how the home front leaped to man the factories, and how our fighting men in the air, on the sea and on the land carried the fight to the enemy is indeed an inspiring story.

Truly global in scope, massive in manpower and destruction, rich in heroic deed, and scarred with countless examples of man's inhumanity to man, the Second World War has been written about by historians, playwrights, and novelists. Yet most of these authors suffered from the myopia of being participants in the events described or have looked at the war from the sole viewpoint of one or another of the combatants. Now, a Swiss military historian, Lt. Colonel Eddy Bauer, has clearly and without the bias of involvement, set forth, as impartially as any one writer can, the tremendous story of millions of men and women surging in battle across continents.

Colonel Bauer, from the depths of his profound study and his understanding of humanity, has produced an extraordinarily well balanced account of the conflict. His story, illuminated by many maps and enlivened with authentic pictures of the times, many in color and only recently discovered, sharpens and deepens our awareness of the conflict and makes clear the forces driving the strategies, the tactics, and even the individuals of the nations at war. To understand these, free from ideological bias, is to understand better how to avoid a future cataclysm. Pearl Harbor, Bataan, and Corregidor, Kasserine and Cassino, the Solomons and Leyte Gulf, Normandy and The Ardennes, Okinawa and Iwo Jima are stamped on American memories as deeply as are Stalingrad and the Battle of Britain on the minds of other participants. A group of distinguished scholars has undertaken to amplify and deepen Colonel Bauer's treatment of those phases of transcendent American interest. Perhaps I am showing my American bias, but I feel that these additions strengthen and improve the work. I also think that Colonel Bauer would approve had he lived to see the complete opus in print.

You now have the opportunity to visit or revisit the Second World War through The Marshall Cavendish ILLUSTRATED ENCYCLOPEDIA OF WORLD WAR II. This lavishly presented, clearly written, judicious work brings the war alive through thousands of full color photographs and is made even more interesting due to the emphasis put on those aspects of greatest concern to Americans.

James L. Collins Jr

JAMES L. COLLINS, JR.
Brigadier General, USA

THE GREAT BETRAYAL

◁ *How central Europe was re-shaped by the Treaty of Versailles. Promising flashpoints included the demilitarised Rhineland, the "Polish Corridor" separating East Prussia from Germany, and the regions of Slovakia claimed by Hungary—not to mention Italy's dissatisfaction at not gaining Dalmatia and the whole of the South Tyrol.*
▷ *After the Austrian Anschluss: Arthur Seyss-Inquart, key Nazi in the takeover of Austria, with Bormann, Kaltenbrunner, Hitler, Himmler, and Heydrich.*
▽ ▷ *The newly-promoted Field-Marshal Göring, chief of the Luftwaffe, reviews Austrian recruits for his air force in Vienna.*

grievance would lead to World War II.

Rhineland, 1936: Hitler's first gamble

In the Locarno Treaty of 1925 the Allies undertook to evacuate the Rhineland in 1930 for a German guarantee not to remilitarise it. When Adolf Hitler became German Chancellor in 1933 he declared that he would abide by the terms of the treaty, but in reality he was waiting only for a suitable excuse to bring the Rhineland "home to the Reich". Such an excuse arrived on March 2, 1935, when France and Soviet Russia came to a preliminary agreement for a mutual aid pact.

On March 16 Hitler abolished the military restraints of the Versailles "*diktat*", proclaiming conscription for an enlarged German Army and a new German Air Force or Luftwaffe. In a speech to the Reichstag on May 21, Hitler announced that any fears of renewed aggression by Germany were totally unfounded; but in an audience with the French Ambassador, François-Poncet, on November 21 he declared that the conditions of the Locarno Treaty would be made void by the formal ratification of a Franco-Soviet pact. François-Poncet immediately warned the French Government that this was a clear indication that Hitler intended to reoccupy the Rhineland, but the warning went unheeded.

Pending the ratification of the Franco-Soviet pact the German General Staff, on Hitler's orders, prepared plans for the Rhineland coup. The small German Army of 1936 was no match for the French Army alone, and the German

Versailles, 1919: Seed-bed of discontent

On June 28, 1919, the Treaty of Versailles was signed and World War I came to its official end. The Treaty had a twofold purpose: to confine defeated Germany territorially, and to lay down the frontiers of the new states created from the ruins of the Tsarist Russian Empire and Austria-Hungary.

The Treaty gave Germany two lasting grievances with regard to her frontiers: the new rights of France to use the Saar coalfields and to garrison the Rhineland, demilitarised by Germany; and the severance of East Prussia from Germany by the "Danzig Corridor" granted to Poland. Immense financial reparations were imposed on Germany by the victors of World War I, so heavy that they would have crippled Germany for decades if they had been paid in full. To crown everything, Germany's army and navy were cut down to the minimum and she was forbidden to build warplanes, tanks, or submarines.

When the details were set out in the subsequent treaties of Trianon and St. Germain, few of the states on the new map of Europe were satisfied with what they had been given. Poland had further claims against Russia and Czechoslovakia, Hungary against Czechoslovakia and Rumania, and Italy against Yugoslavia and Austria. Minorities such as the Croats in Yugoslavia also had their own separatist movements, and there were German minorities in Poland, Czechoslovakia, and Alsace-Lorraine.

The Treaty of Versailles could not bring peace to Europe. It did too much and too little. Germany was humiliated and, given the right conditions, would seek revenge. The new states of Europe and smaller minorities within them still had scores to settle. Step by step, these twin sources of

generals believed that the British would join the French in armed intervention against Germany. Field-Marshal Werner von Blomberg, German War Minister, gave orders that if the French opposed the reoccupation the German troops were to pull back immediately. He considered it better to admit defeat if Hitler's bluff were called.

The Franco-Soviet Pact was ratified on February 27, 1936, and on March 1 Hitler made his decision to act. On the 7th the German troops went in, to be greeted with wild enthusiasm by the German civilian population of the Rhineland. There was absolutely no opposition. The French did not march; the British refused to take the initiative.

Hitler had gained not only a valuable military advantage but also an important moral victory over his cautious staff officers. But most significant of all was the apathy and hesitation displayed by France and Britain. This knowledge would be an immense help to Hitler over the next three years.

Austria, March 1938: "Greater Germany" is born

A Nazi takeover of Austria had always been an essential part of Hitler's programme to unite the German people. After his rise to power in Germany there was much support for Hitler in Austria, but this slumped considerably after a badly-timed Nazi coup was suppressed in Vienna during July

Ein Volk, ein Reich, ein Führer!

VOLK WILL ZU VOLK
UND BLUT ZU BLUT
DEM FÜHRER DEIN Ja

△ *The drumbeat slogan of Hitler's Germany: "One People, one Reich, one Führer!"*
▷ *Hitler and other Nazi V.I.P.s listen to a speech by Sudeten party leader Konrad Henlein.*
▽ *"People to people; blood to blood"–a poster hailing the union of Austria with Germany in the* Anschluss *of 1938.*

1934. During the coup the Austrian Chancellor, Dollfuss, had been assassinated. His successor, Schuschnigg, determinedly continued with a policy of independence from Nazi Germany, under the patronage of France and Italy.

Austria's position began to alter radically after 1936. She lost her two main props, France and Italy, the former as a result of her internal troubles and the latter of the Axis agreement, the Nazi-Fascist accord of that year. Austria's isolation and the growing strength of the German Wehrmacht, now about to undergo its first taste of action in the Spanish Civil War, led Hitler to renew German pressure for unification with Austria. Schuschnigg remained adamant that this should not take place, but Hitler made his position brutally clear in a meeting at Berchtesgaden in February 1938. If the Austrian Nazi movement were not legalised immediately and given a major rôle in the Austrian government, the German Army would invade Austria and impose these con-

ditions by force. Deprived of the support of France and Italy, Schuschnigg attempted to thwart Hitler's plans by holding a plebiscite to decide Austria's future, but was in turn defeated by Hitler's ultimatum of immediate invasion if the plebiscite were not called off and Schuschnigg replaced as Chancellor by the Austrian Nazi leader, Dr. Arthur Seyss-Inquart. Schuschnigg resigned on March 11 and was duly replaced by Seyss-Inquart, whose first act on the 12th was to send a prearranged telegram asking for the German Army to be sent into Austria "to establish peace and order . . . and to pre-

vent bloodshed". On the 13th Seyss-Inquart declared *Anschluss* (annexation) by Germany. Austria was Austria no more, but the *Ostmark* of the "Greater German Reich".

In 1935 Hitler had defied the military restrictions imposed on Germany by the Allies in 1919. In 1936 he had reoccupied a part of Germany taken from her in 1919. With the *Anschluss* of March 1938 he had seized Austria in defiance of her separation from Germany in 1919. He had already selected his next victim: Czechoslovakia, now hemmed in by German territory on three sides.

...choslovakia

...g the
...ia,

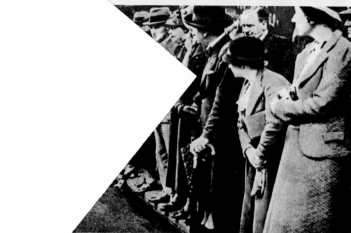

si...
mach...
the Sude...
secuted min...
Reich as their ...
encouraged the a...
Sudetendeutsche Pa...
Konrad Henlein, which ...
for unification with Germa...

In May 1938 Hitler decided ...
annex the Sudetenland and German divisions began to move into
position for a military takeover—
but France, Britain, and Soviet
Russia all announced that a German invasion of Czechoslovakia
would elicit an immediate military
response, and Hitler was forced to
back down. Throughout the summer the Nazis engineered repeated
"incidents" in the Sudetenland,
which Hitler used as his excuse
that the plight of the Sudeten Germans must be settled as soon as
possible. On September 12, he
wound up the 1938 Nuremberg
Rally in which he insisted on "self-
determination" for the Sudetenland and hurled insults and threats
at Prague. The result was a revolt,
ruthlessly crushed by the Prague
Government of President Beneš,
in the Sudetenland.

At this point the diplomatic
impasse was broken by Britain's
Prime Minister, Neville Chamberlain, who expressed his desire to
discuss a peaceful settlement with
Hitler. After the first meeting
between Hitler and Chamberlain,
at Berchtesgaden on September
15, the French and British con-
ferred and informed President
Beneš that if he chose to go to war
over the Sudetenland France and
Britain would not stand by him.
At Bad Godesberg, on the 22nd,
Chamberlain told Hitler that his
claim on the Sudetenland would
be met, but Hitler replied that this
was no longer enough: German
troops must go in at once. This

Chamberlain refused to countenance. The Czechs mobilised on
September 23, and with the British
and French governments refusing
to grant Hitler's latest demands,
war was imminent. But then
Chamberlain broke the deadlock,
by suggesting a last-minute conference with Italy as mediator.

So it was that Hitler, Mussolini,
and the French and British Prime
Ministers, Edouard Daladier and
Chamberlain, gathered in Munich
on September 29, 1938. Soviet
Russia and Czechoslovakia were
not consulted. Britain and France
backed down entirely from their
previous position, and agreed that
Germany could start occupying
the Sudetenland from October 1
(the date that Hitler had already
fixed as the day of the German invasion if diplomacy failed) in return for Hitler's guarantee that
this was his "last territorial demand in Europe". Britain and
France had betrayed Czecho-
slovakia for an empty promise that
they naïvely believed would bring
"peace in our time".

Jan Masaryk, Czech Minister
in London and the son of Czecho-
slovakia's founding father, called
on Chamberlain on the eve of his
departure for the Munich Conference. "If you have sacrificed my
nation to preserve the peace of the
world," he said, "I will be the first
to applaud you. But if not, gentlemen, God help your souls!"

△ ...tred in the Sudetenland: a synagogue burns,
firea... ...nlein's thugs. . . In London, an apathetic queue
declines pro-Czech leaflets. Britain's refusal to "Stand by the
Czechs" robbed Chamberlain's peace of honour at Munich.
▽ Roses, roses all the way—ecstatic Sudeten Germans fête
occupying German troops with Nazi banners, cheers, bouquets,
and adoring girls as the Sudetenland comes "home to the Reich"
after Munich.

Nun haben wir wieder eine glückliche Zukunft!

Ja

dafür danken wir dem Führer am 4. Dezember

dein **Ja**

dem **Führer** am **4. Dezember**

Ganz Deutschland hört den Führer

mit dem Volksempfänger

Zug um Zug zerriß Adolf Hitler das Diktat v. Versailles!

1933 Deutschland verläßt den Völkerbund von Versailles!

1934 Der Wiederaufbau der Wehrmacht, der Kriegsmarine und der Luftwaffe wird eingeleitet!

1935 Saargebiet heimgeholt! Wehrhoheit des Reiches wiedergewonnen!

1936 Rheinland vollständig befreit!

1937 Kriegsschuldlüge feierlich ausgelöscht!

1938 Deutsch-Oesterreich dem Reiche angeschlossen! Großdeutschland verwirklicht!

Darum bekennt sich ganz Deutschland am 10. April zu seinem Befreier

Adolf Hitler

Alle sagen: **Ja!**

△ Two posters circulated in the Sudetenland after the German occupation, urging a solid Nazi vote in the rubber-stamp Reichstag election on December 4, 1938. ◁ ◁ "All Germany hears the Führer"–radio was one of the most potent weapons in the propaganda armoury of Goebbels. ◁ How the Nazis exploited the legacy of Versailles, hailing the successive steps by which Hitler made a mockery of the Treaty. ▷ The face of honesty confronted with evil–Neville Chamberlain at Bad Godesberg.

CHAPTER I
MUNICH: the morning after

On New Year's Day, 1939, the Papal Nuncio, Monsignor Valerio Valeri, doyen of the *corps diplomatique* in Paris, came to the Elysée Palace to pay his respects and those of his colleagues to the President of the French Republic. Monsignor Valeri expressed his hope that the New Year would see peace maintained throughout Europe and the world. Replying, President Albert Lebrun endorsed these sentiments in the name of France. No doubt both men were speaking with complete sincerity, but it is hard to imagine that they expected to be exchanging the same wishes on New Year's Day, 1940.

Nevertheless, it seemed as though there might be grounds for hope. On December 6, 1938, the French and German Foreign Ministers, Georges Bonnet and Joachim von Ribbentrop, had met in Paris and signed a declaration which, following the Munich agreement of the same year, seemed on the face of it to promise an end to the traditional hostility between the two countries.

It was a move which the British Government had encouraged in the tense weeks since Munich. In their joint declaration, France and Germany expressed their conviction that "peaceful and neighbourly relations between Germany and France form one of the essential elements in the consolidation of the European situation, as well as in the general maintenance of peace". Bonnet did not regard this document as an empty "scrap of paper": Article 2 expressed the mutual agreement that no territorial disputes between France and Germany remained, and that both countries "solemnly regarded the existing frontier between their countries as the definitive frontier". Although those provinces were not mentioned by name, Ribbentrop's signature on this freely-contracted agreement prevented Germany from ever again laying a legal claim to Alsace and Lorraine. After the signature of the agreement, Ribbentrop said to Bonnet: "Do not forget that the renunciation of Alsace and Lorraine which I have just made in the name of Germany is a very sensitive point as far as our national self-esteem is concerned."

The French diplomats could also congratulate themselves in that Article 3 expressly stated that France's existing international commitments were not affected. The most important were the Franco-Polish Treaty of 1921 and the Franco-Soviet Pact of 1936. Neither Lukasiewicz, Polish Ambassador to Paris, nor Suritz, the Soviet Ambassador, raised any objections to France's new agreement with Germany. Also in Article 3, France and Germany declared their willingness to "discuss all questions concerning their two countries, and to consult each other whenever one of these questions theatens to lead to international difficulties".

"Once the Sudeten problem is settled . . ."

So it was that in Paris it almost seemed that Hitler and Ribbentrop really had abandoned their policy of armed coups and unilateral expansion which had threatened to set Europe ablaze three times in the last three years.

Events were indeed to prove how futile such hopes were; but in every capital in Europe people still vividly remembered Adolf Hitler's raucous voice announcing from the Berlin Sportpalast on September 26, 1938: "Once the Sudeten problem is settled no territorial problem in Europe will remain. It is the last territorial demand I have to make in Europe. This I guarantee. We want no Czechs at all." Hitler had said the same to British Prime Minister Neville Chamberlain during their meeting at Bad Godesberg on September 22, and Chamberlain had been convinced. He had returned to England to announce: "I think I should add that [Hitler] repeated to me with great earnestness what he had said already at Berchtesgaden, namely, that this was the last of his territorial ambitions in Europe and that he had no wish to include in the Reich people of other races than Germans. In the second place he said, again very earnestly, that he wanted to be friends with England and that if only this Sudeten question could be got out of the way in peace he would gladly resume conversations. It is true he said, 'There is one

HOW THEY SOLD OUT

CZECHOSLOVAKIA

We, the German Führer and Chancellor and the British Prime Minister, have had a further meeting today and are agreed in recognising that the question of Anglo-German relations is of the first importance for the two countries and for Europe.

We regard the agreement signed last night and the Anglo-German Naval Agreement as symbolic of the desire of our two peoples never to go to war with one another again.

We are resolved that the method of consultation shall be the method adopted to deal with any other questions that may concern our two countries, and we are determined to continue our efforts to remove possible sources of difference and thus to contribute to assure the peace of Europe.

September 30. 1938.

1. *Teacups and tension: at Bad Godesberg, Chamberlain and Hitler discuss the Sudeten territory claimed by Germany, with interpreter Schmidt and British Ambassador to Berlin, Sir Nevile Henderson, at right.* **2.** *When ignorance is bliss: Chamberlain at Munich. The Prime Minister was naïvely pleased with the carefully stage-managed receptions which he was given in Germany.* **3.** *Cartoonist David Low depicts Stalin as asking "What, no seat for me?" at the time of the Munich crisis. The Russians, like the Czechs themselves, were excluded from the Munich talks.* **4.** *French cartoon of the Munich "peace-pipe" conference – surrounded by explosives.* **5-6-7.** *Putting the final signature on the document which tore the Sudetenland from Czechoslovakia – Chamberlain, Hitler, and Mussolini.* **8.** *On his return to Britain, Chamberlain brandishes the paper which he believed meant "peace in our time" – the declaration of Anglo-German concord* **(9)** *which he and Hitler signed the morning after the Munich settlement of September 29, 1938.*

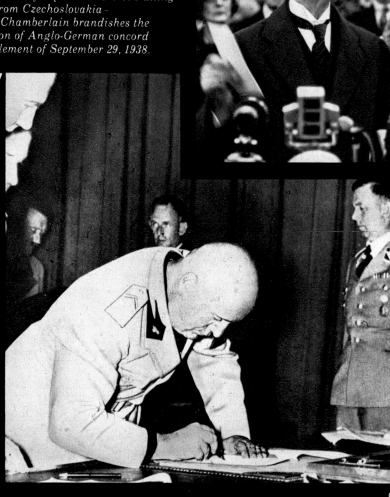

△ *On the Czech frontier, Polish officers discuss the occupation of the Teschen region ceded to Poland by Czechoslovakia.*
▽ *Easy winnings for Poland: a jubilant General Malinowski embraces an elderly countrywoman during the Polish take-over.*

awkward question, the Colonies . . . but that is not a matter for war.' "

Naturally, in January 1939 neither the French nor the British had at their disposal the vast, incriminating mass of documents which would be laid before the International Military Tribunal at Nuremberg in 1946. But even in January 1939 there were men in high places who were not completely blind to the dangers of the situation, or to the possibility of the Third Reich once again breaking its pledged word and engineering another coup.

Nor did Hitler's Germany stand alone: it was aligned with the Italian Fascist Empire created by Benito Mussolini. Together the two dictatorships formed the "Berlin-Rome Axis", a grandiose concept which Mussolini had outlined in November 1936. He saw the "Axis" as a polarising influence around which the other European countries "may work together". Whether or not this would happen had yet to be seen; but there was no denying the importance of the Axis after Munich.

The Munich agreement had been signed on September 29, 1938. One of its clauses had stipulated that an international guarantee of Czechoslovakia's future security be given by each of the contracting powers. As far as France and Great Britain were concerned, this guarantee was the essential condition for their agreeing to the dissection of Czechoslovakia. It was a substitute for the natural strategic frontiers which the surrender of the Sudetenland to Germany had torn from Czechoslovakia. The same guarantee would be required from Germany and

Italy – on one condition. As Article 1 of the agreement put it, "when the question of the Polish and Hungarian minorities in Czechoslovakia has been settled, Germany and Italy will each give a similar guarantee to Czechoslovakia". Poland had been first to share the spoils. After an ultimatum from Warsaw on September 27, 1938, Czechoslovakia had ceded to Poland the district of Těšín (Teschen) – some 625 square miles with a population of 230,000.

Hungary takes her share

With Poland satisfied, the thorny problem of the Hungarian claims remained. Both sides negotiated at Komárno for a "direct agreement" to put an end to the national and territorial disputes stemming from the Treaty of Trianon in 1920. After four days of discussion – or rather recrimination – neither side had given way. Hungary would willingly have gone to war to settle the problem but Germany and Italy intervened, and the governments of Prague and Budapest submitted to their arbitration.

On November 2, 1938, the Czech and Hungarian Foreign Ministers, František Chvalkovský and Kálmán Kánya, met in the sumptuous Belvedere Palace in Vienna. After both parties had pleaded their respective cases the Axis arbitrators, Ribbentrop and Count Galeazzo Ciano, the Italian Foreign Minister, retired to consider their verdict. After much disagreement they announced their joint decision: "to allot to Hungary those territorial zones which otherwise could well have become the objects of numerous bitter disputes".

The sentence of Vienna did not satisfy Hungary's aspirations to all of Sub-Carpathian Ruthenia, but she still got the districts of Mukačevo, Užhorod, Košice, Lučenec, Levice, and Nové Zámky (in all an area of 7,500 square miles with a population of 775,000). This left Czechoslovakia with only one city on the Danube: Bratislava, capital of Slovakia. All ceded territories, it was announced, must be evacuated by November 10.

This compromise aroused great indignation in Budapest, and Hitler and Mussolini were hard put to it to prevent the Hungarians from using force to secure the provinces which had been denied them. Nor was it any better received in Bratislava, where the Slovak leaders accused the Prague Government of having sold them out in agreeing to the dismemberment of their lands. This completely overshadowed the new measures of autonomy granted to the Slovaks by the Czech Government in Prague – a concession which now officially hyphenated the country as Czecho-Slovakia.

The Slovaks did not know that during the Italo-German arbitration in Vienna the unfortunate Chvalkovský had managed to whisper in Ciano's ear: "I will have to resign tomorrow. No government could survive such a shock." But back in Prague, where a new government with Rudolf Beran as Prime Minister had taken over on October 7, the administration found or thought it had found some measure of compensation in the whole deplorable arrangement.

Having appeased the Polish and Hungarian demands in accordance with the Munich agreement, Czecho-Slovakia was now entitled to ask for the promised guarantees from Italy and Germany. On November 5 Chvalkovský raised the point in a discussion with Dr. Hencke, German *chargé d'affaires* in Prague, only to get the reply: "The question of the guarantee will not arise until the new frontiers have been defined in detail by the commissions."

This had been done by November 20, but when a Czech official raised the point again Hencke had no scruples in replying that "the question of the guarantee had no direct connection with the settlement of the frontiers". This was not Ciano's view. He saw no reason for evading the Czech request, but when he gave his opinion that Germany would acquiesce "readily", it is obvious that Ribbentrop had led his Italian opposite number into a fool's paradise.

Evasive double-talk, German style

After this significant piece of evasion by the Germans, Ribbentrop's visit to Paris in early December to sign the Franco-German declaration gave Georges Bonnet an excellent opportunity to put his oar in. But when the conversation came round to Czecho-Slovakia and the German guarantee, all Ribbentrop gave Bonnet was an ambiguous reply which gave the latter much food for thought. First, he said, Germany was going to see how things went. Second, a four-power guarantee would only "encourage" the Prague Government to return to the "errors" of ex-President Eduard Beneš (who had resigned on October 5) – by which he meant relying on support from France, Britain, and the Soviet Union in the event of pressure from Germany.

Despite this rebuff, so lightly wrapped up in diplomatic double-talk, the French Cabinet tried again. Its new spokesman was Ambassador Robert Coulondre, who had just been transferred from Moscow to Berlin. On December 21, 1938, Coulondre carried out his orders to raise the subject of the joint guarantee with German Secretary of State Baron Ernst von Weizsäcker. The latter, however, repeated

△ *November 2, 1938: the climax of the axis arbitration between Czechoslovakia and Hungary in the Belvedere Palace, Vienna. Ribbentrop, with Ciano seated on his right, reads the Axis verdict, defining the regions of Slovakia to be handed over to the Hungarians. Kálmán Kánya, Hungary's Foreign Minister* (extreme right) *listens dourly: the Axis arbitrations did not meet Hungary's claims in full.*

the evasive gambit: "Czecho-Slovakia is not pressing the point, and the Czech Foreign Minister will not be coming to Berlin until after the holidays. There is no hurry."

This was rather an insidious answer, since if Prague had made no official request for the guarantee to Berlin it was only because the first tentative approaches made by Chvalkovský had met with such an unpromising attitude on the part of Hencke.

Needless to say the French Foreign Ministry was not deceived by Weizsäcker's reply. All the evidence now showed that the Munich agreement had not put an end to Hitler's ambitions, despite his solemn protestations to the contrary. All that Munich had done was to give Hitler a springboard for further advances. The suspicions of French Prime Minister Edouard Daladier and Bonnet would have been amply confirmed if they could have seen the Directive of October 21, 1938, in which Hitler had ordered the Wehrmacht to prepare for the final liquidation of "the remainder of Czecho-Slovakia".

Under these conditions, what remained of the Franco-German "joint declaration" of December 6? André François-Poncet, the retiring Ambassador, had returned from a farewell audience with Hitler at Berchtesgaden on October 18. With some apprehension, he wrote: "If these undertakings are kept they will considerably relieve the tension in Europe. But if they are broken, the guilty party will have a heavy moral responsibility to bear."

Isolation for America

Across the Atlantic, the American Congress reflected two sentiments, each contradicting the other. One sector of opinion was deeply opposed to the totalitarian, racist dictatorships which had arisen in Europe; the other condemned American involvement in Europe in any shape or form.

This was underlined by the excitement caused by a speech made by William Bullitt, American Ambassador to France, on September 4, 1938. If war should break out in Europe, he said, it would be impossible to say whether or not the United States would become involved. Cautious as it was, this statement caused a furore in the United States, and Roosevelt felt himself obliged to make a public dis-

△ *The disease of Nazi Germany: a cartoon condemning the machinations of "the eternal Jew".* ◁ *Herschel Grynszpan, the crazed young Jew whose assassination of Ernst vom Rath in Paris triggered off the destructive "Week of Broken Glass" in Germany.* ▷ *The debris of the pogrom–smashed Jewish shop windows.*

avowal of Bullitt's words. On September 9, 1939, he reassured the American press. That the United States would side with France and Great Britain against Germany, he declared, was "one hundred per cent" impossible.

Britain: a new note of criticism

What were Britain's feelings in the New Year of 1939?

In describing the Munich agreement to the House of Commons, Neville Chamberlain expressed his belief that an end to surprise military coups had been reached, and that "an era of peace" stretched ahead. The House seemed to have rewarded him with a verdict of 366 Conservative votes against 144 Labour and Liberal votes. But Chamberlain's triumph was far from complete. It was marred by the protest resignation of Duff Cooper, First Lord of the Admiralty. Quite apart from the outspoken lambasting by Winston Churchill—"We have sustained a total and unmitigated defeat"—Chamberlain had to swallow the abstention of 40-odd Members who until Munich had been staunch party supporters.

For all that, Chamberlain's position would remain secure so long as Hitler kept to the terms of the Munich agreement and of the Anglo-German declaration which had followed it. Hitler, however, saw things in a very different light. There existed in Great Britain, he claimed, a clique hostile to peace. If this clique should come to power there would be another world war. For this reason, he announced on October 9, he had decided to extend the fortified zone of the *Westwall* or "Siegfried Line" to include Saarbrücken and Aachen.

Above all, he added: "It would be well for people in Great Britain to start abandoning the superior airs which they have given themselves since the time of Versailles. We will no longer tolerate as we have in the past the interference of British governesses. Enquiries by British politicians concerning Germans within the Reich—*or any peoples dependent upon the Reich*—are misplaced. For our part, we do not concern ourselves with what happens in Britain."

Despite this affront, the German Ambassador in London, Herbert von Dirksen, reported to the Wilhelmstrasse that Chamberlain retained his "complete confidence in the Führer". He followed the same policy of appeasement towards Mussolini. Many politicians in close contact with the Prime Minister felt the same. In particular, Sir Samuel Hoare, the Home Secretary, held that discussions for the limitation of aerial weapons and the "humanising" of war, by the proscription of poison gas and of the bombing of large towns and cities, would be generally welcomed by British public opinion.

The question of the colonies had already been touched upon, but it was obvious that this point would arouse determined opposition from many important quarters. In any case, Chamberlain wondered if this tricky problem really could be tackled now, or "if it would not be better to wait until the German Government has found a satisfactory solution to the urgent problems raised by the cession of the the Sudetenland to the Reich and the new pattern of relations between Czecho-Slovakia and her neighbours".

Less than three weeks later, on November 17, Dirksen was writing that Chamberlain was no longer in the least disposed to reopen negotiations with Germany on the lines proposed at Munich. In his report to Ribbentrop on that day, Dirksen suggested two reasons for this.

First, the many invitations for negotiations made in speeches by Chamberlain, Foreign Secretary Lord Halifax, and Hoare had been completely ignored by Berlin. From this the British Cabinet could only conclude that Hitler and Ribbentrop had no interest whatsoever in seeing Anglo-German relations improved.

The second reason was the revulsion caused by a new and vicious pogrom in Germany. On November 7, in Paris, a young Jew named Herschel Grynszpan had assassinated a secretary of the German Legation, Ernst vom Rath, in protest against the deportation to Poland of German Jews. Hideous reprisals were taken against Jews in the Reich. In the "Week of Broken Glass", which began on the night of November 9–10, the régime had encouraged the most brutal excesses on the part of the German populace. In correct diplomatic language—but with a clarity which left nothing in doubt—Ambassador Dirksen told Ribbentrop of the deep impression which this brutal pogrom had made on every sector of British public opinion. The opponents of appeasement, who had never ceased to

△ *"Don't buy from Jews!"– anti-Semitic propaganda during the pogrom of November 1938. Burly, brown-shirted thugs barring shop entrances, and insulting Nazi Party placards in the windows, brought despair and ruin to many a Jewish business in Hitler's Germany.*

▽ *The most effective propaganda of all: destruction. German police and firemen, summoned to a blazing synagogue in November 1938, display their patriotism as good Germans by waiting until the flames have finished the job for them.*

condemn the Munich agreement, had been immensely strengthened in their attacks upon Chamberlain's Government, while the supporters of an Anglo-German *rapprochement* – "morally very hard hit" – had been reduced to silence.

Dirksen added: "If this atmosphere persists it will be impossible for Chamberlain to hope for success in his plan of reaching a secure agreement with Germany." Even worse, he added (without actually saying that this was his view), "many well-informed personalities" believed that the Prime Minister was in fact revising his assessment of the future of Anglo-German relations.

Chamberlain had indeed felt affronted by Hitler's speech on October 9. In particular the offensive reference to "British governesses" stuck in Chamberlain's throat. Apart from that, the silence which had greeted his suggestions for co-operation and disarmament had seemed to be a bad omen for the future. Despite this, however, Chamberlain had not yet despaired of his hopes for world peace.

When it came down to it, the Munich settlement had prevented a direct clash between France and Germany in which Great Britain must have been involved as well. Certainly Britain could never remain a passive observer of a defeat of France without endangering her own security, both in north-western Europe and in the Mediterranean.

Once he was master of the Continent and had disarmed the defeated states, Hitler could reduce his land forces to a level in proportion with the military strength of the Soviet Union. He could then use the industrial potential thus made available to begin a large-scale programme of warship construction which would in time threaten the Royal Navy's numerical lead. This was why Chamberlain and Halifax were somewhat relieved to hear the news, on December 6, that a new "joint declaration", not unlike the one signed by Hitler and Chamberlain in Munich on September 30, had been issued in Paris by Ribbentrop and Bonnet.

War had been averted in north-western Europe, but another flashpoint still glowed in the western Mediterranean. It was intensified by Italy's denunciation of the Laval-Mussolini agreements of 1935 (in which France had agreed not to obstruct Italian colonial expansion), and by the incredible anti-French propaganda campaign launched by the Italian Fascist Government.

On November 30, 1938, Mussolini addressed the Fascist Grand Council. He outlined the majority of Italy's "claims" and, in his personal style, went on to add some more. "I will now describe to you," he told the Council, "the next objectives in the Fascist programme. As Adowa [Italy's defeat in Abyssinia in 1896] has been avenged in Abyssinia, so will we avenge Valona [Italy's expulsion from Albania in 1920]. Albania will become Italian. I cannot and will not tell you when or how. But so it will be. And for our security in this Mediterranean world which surrounds us, we must have Tunisia and Corsica. Our frontier with France must be extended to the Var. I do not aspire to Savoy, for it lies beyond the Alps. But instead I am thinking of the Ticino, for Switzerland has lost her cohesion and, like several other small states, is destined for partition one day.

"All this constitutes our programme. I cannot give you a definite date for its completion: I am only outlining the objectives . . ."

Daladier's dagger

In order to counter these Italian claims and the anti-French press campaign which followed at Mussolini's direct instigation, Edouard Daladier made a whistle-stop tour of Corsica, Tunisia, and the other French territories in North Africa. "We will never," he asserted during his journey, "yield an inch of territory which belongs to us." That word "never" provoked renewed fury from the Fascist propagandists. But worse was to come. At Ajaccio in Corsica, as was the custom, a presentation dagger was given to the French statesman. Daladier jokingly brandished the dagger, made a ferocious face, and transfixed an imaginary foe. The scene was captured by the camera and was published by the Italian press with fearful imprecations. Daladier was threatening Italy with his dagger! He was defying Italy!

War between France and Italy seemed more than likely, for – quite reasonably – France was certainly not going to yield to Italy's ambition of spreading her empire across the whole of North Africa and of turning the western Mediterranean into an Italian lake. But could such a conflict be localised if it broke out? London thought not. It was to be hoped that

DUBLIN
EIRE

March 15, 193
Anschluss
(Austria annexe

Santander

Oporto

PORTUGAL

LISBON
Tagus

MADRID

SPAIN

Seville

Granada

GIBRALTAR

Tangiers

14

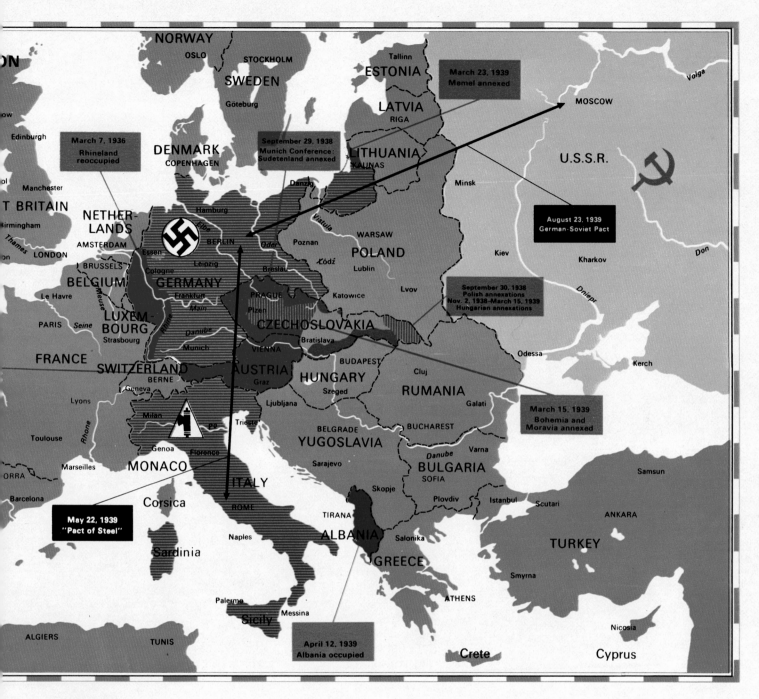

Map labels:

- March 7, 1936 — Rhineland reoccupied
- September 29, 1938 — Munich Conference: Sudetenland annexed
- March 23, 1939 — Memel annexed
- August 23, 1939 — German-Soviet Pact
- September 30, 1938 Polish annexations / Nov. 2, 1938–March 15, 1939 Hungarian annexations
- March 15, 1939 — Bohemia and Moravia annexed
- May 22, 1939 — "Pact of Steel"
- April 12, 1939 — Albania occupied

Hitler would curb Mussolini, but this was no real guarantee that Mussolini would not go to war of his own accord. If it came to a fight, the advantage would definitely lie with France. Yet no one seriously believed that Hitler would allow his sole friend and ally in Europe to be defeated–and if Hitler went to Mussolini's aid Britain would have to intervene too.

London was therefore most anxious to pour oil on these troubled waters. On April 16, 1938, a protocol had settled the differences between Italy and Great Britain in the Mediterranean, East Africa, and the Middle East on the basis of the *status quo*. Once this agreement was in force, Chamberlain thought he could intervene both in Rome and in Paris.

Speaking in the House of Commons on December 14, 1938, he made his attitude to both sides quite clear: "In the view of His Majesty's Government, the undertaking to respect the *status quo* in the Mediterranean, as embodied in the Anglo-Italian Agreement, certainly applies to Tunis." In addition, Chamberlain's visit to Rome (January 11–13, 1939) seemed intended to caution Mussolini to revise his anti-French policy.

Such was Britain's attitude in January 1939. Chamberlain had come a long way from the euphoria in which he had returned from Munich, but his honest naïveté still prevented him from expecting the worst from a man who had signed a declaration of Anglo-German friendship.

15

CHAPTER 2
PRAGUE: brutal awakening

△ After his new coup in March 1939, Hitler enters Prague in triumph. Hitler had been heard to criticise Chamberlain after Munich: "That fellow has spoiled my entry into Prague!" But the Führer only had to wait five and a half months before getting his wish.

"A conqueror always likes peace," Clausewitz had written in his notes *On War*; "he would prefer to invade us without meeting resistance." By January 1939 the three great coups of the Third Reich – the reoccupation of the Rhineland, the Austrian *Anschluss*, and the seizure of the Czech Sudetenland – had proved that Adolf Hitler was adept at making realities out of this theory. But the events of the four months after the Munich agreement – October 1938–January 1939 – had shown that Hitler was an innovator in another sense. He had invented the modern concept of the "Cold War", the "Phoney Peace", using the troubles and tensions of the world to get what he wanted without fighting wars. Of all Hitler's inventions, the Cold War was the one which was to outlive him longest.

As early as autumn 1937 Hitler could look back on an impressive list of successes. These included the dissolution of the Franco-British-Italian "Stresa Front" (the last alignment of World War I's Allies against Germany), formed in 1935

after Hitler's announcement of German rearmament and the reintroduction of conscription in Germany. Moreover, the Spanish Civil War was increasing the already bitter differences between Fascist Italy and Republican France. But when Hitler considered his next move – the incorporation into the Reich of Austria and Czechoslovakia – he knew for sure that he was running the risk of a major war.

With this in mind, Hitler had called a meeting of top-ranking officials and commanders in the New Chancellery on November 5, 1937. Those present included Field-Marshal Werner von Blomberg, the War Minister; Colonel-General Freiherr Werner von Fritsch, Commander-in-Chief of the Army; General Hermann Göring, Commander-in-Chief of the Luftwaffe; Grand-Admiral Erich Raeder, Commander-in-Chief of the Navy; Baron Konstantin von Neurath, Foreign Minister – and Colonel Friedrich Hossbach, military adjutant to the Führer, whose detailed notes of what Hitler had to say at this meeting were to play an important rôle at the Nuremberg Tribunal after the war.

Some historians have questioned both the accuracy and the validity of the "Hossbach Memorandum". However, Hossbach himself was no fool (he ended up as an army commander on the Eastern Front). What he recorded in his Memorandum was not a detailed war blueprint: it was not even remotely justified by the actual course of events. It shows Hitler thinking aloud, putting the inevitability of war to the leaders of the Wehrmacht.

Hitler began by explaining that the purpose of the meeting was so important that he thought it best not to bring it before the complete Reich Cabinet. "What he was going to say," noted Hossbach, "was the result of profound deliberation and of his four years in power; he would explain to the gentlemen present his basic ideas on the opportunities and the requirements for the basic growth of our external political situation. As a result, he asked that in the interest of Germany's long-term political future they should be regarded as his last will and testament in the event of his death."

Hitler continued: "The aim of German policy is to secure and protect the racial community [*Volksmasse*] and to enlarge it. It is therefore a question of living space [*Lebensraum*]."

Having established these principles, Hitler went on to describe the economic opportunities offered to a nation of 85 million Germans – a figure including Austrians and Sudeten Germans, with an annual birth-rate put at 560,000. He then outlined Germany's most obvious needs: non-ferrous metals for industrial expansion, and increased food supplies.

Could these serious deficiencies be made good by trade? Hitler thought not, for two reasons: too many countries, former exporters of foodstuffs, had become industrialised since 1918; and the development of Germany's overseas trade (without her former colonies in Africa) would make the Reich dependent upon her two "irreducible enemies" – Great Britain and France.

As a result, Hitler continued: "Only force can solve Germany's problems, and force always has its risks ... if we deliberately resort to force, having accepted these risks, the next questions are 'When?' and 'How?'."

As far as the timing was concerned, Hitler told his audience that the impressive superiority in weapons and equip-

ment at present enjoyed by the Wehrmacht would dwindle, approaching zero after 1943–45. As a result, if he were still alive, Hitler was "irrevocably determined to settle the problem of Germany's living-space by 1943–45 at the latest".

Two conditions, however, could make it necessary for the Third Reich to act before then: if France's social problems became so acute that the French Army had to be called in and became neutralised in the process; or if France got herself so involved in a war with a third power that she could not respond with sufficient force to a German attack. In any event, Germany must seize the chance to deal with Austria and Czechoslovakia. If

Shadow in the sky: poster for a national German air display in 1937. The threat of terror bombings by the Luftwaffe – trained in peace and tempered in the Spanish Civil War – was used to bludgeon the Czech leaders into submission during the crisis of March 1939.

NATIONALSOZIALISTISCHES FLIEGERKORPS

Deutschlandflug 1937

20.-27. JUNI

Grossflugtag auf dem Tempelhofer Feld am 27. Juni 15 Uhr

17

secured "with lightning speed", a German success would deter the Soviet Union and Poland from any serious ideas of intervening. As for Great Britain, who "in all probability" had written off Czechoslovakia", it was extremely unlikely that she would go to war to restore that country's independence, particularly if she were involved with France in a war against Italy.

The acquisition of Austria and Czechoslovakia would, given the right conditions, provide sufficient extra foodstuffs for five to six million Germans. More important, Germany would experience "a great lightening of politico-military burdens by shortening and strengthening the Reich's frontiers. This would enable troops to be released for service elsewhere. It would also give the Reich 12 new divisions for the army, one division for every million inhabitants" thus incorporated into the Reich.

Blomberg and Fritsch protested at once, reminding Hitler of "the need for Germany to avoid having England and France as enemies". They also doubted that a war with Italy would weaken France sufficiently to prevent her from invading the Rhineland. (It should be remembered that

the German Army manoeuvres of September 20–26, 1937, had in fact been planned with the contingency of war with the Soviet Union in mind.) Neurath, in his turn, objected that an Italo-French conflict was more remote than the Führer seemed to think. Hitler, however, rejected all these objections.

Now there could be no doubt: Hitler was determined on war. There was also no doubt of his scanty regard for the German High Command. As he later said to Hans Frank, the Governor-General of conquered Poland: "For years these gentlemen in their fancy red-striped breeches have betrayed, forgotten, or sold out the principles of Moltke and Schlieffen. This presumptuous Junker caste is in reality nothing more than a collection of muddleheads, vacillators, and stuffed shirts."

This was borne out by what happened to the three men who protested on November 5, 1937. Blomberg was dismissed in January 1938, ostensibly because of the scandal caused by his marrying a former prostitute. Fritsch fell the same month, on a trumped-up charge of homosexuality (from which he was honourably acquitted by an army court). On February 4, 1938, Hitler assumed the office of

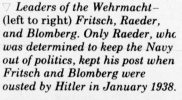

▽ *Leaders of the Wehrmacht– (left to right) Fritsch, Raeder, and Blomberg. Only Raeder, who was determined to keep the Navy out of politics, kept his post when Fritsch and Blomberg were ousted by Hitler in January 1938.*

Commander-in-Chief of the Armed Forces High Command, or "O.K.W." (for *Oberkommando der Wehrmacht*), which now replaced the War Ministry of Blomberg's day. Colonel-General Wilhelm Keitel (an obsequious, unintelligent, but thoroughly reliable yes-man) became Chief-of-Staff. Göring, who had hoped to replace Blomberg, was promoted to Field-Marshal in compensation, while Colonel-General Walter von Brauchitsch replaced Fritsch. Neurath, too, was dismissed from the Foreign Ministry. His place was taken by the vain, conceited Joachim von Ribbentrop, of whom Mussolini said: "You have only to look at his head to see that he has a small brain."

This "palace revolution" gave Hitler complete freedom to go ahead with the programme described in the Hossbach Memorandum. On March 12, 1938, the threat of German armed force enabled him to annex Austria without either a local or a general war. In autumn 1938, however, the intervention of France and Britain forced him to postpone the complete annexation of Czechoslovakia, originally scheduled to coincide with that of Austria. But this was only a partial setback. The Munich agreement gave Hitler all the conditions he would need to complete the liquidation of the Czechoslovak state, once more without having to resort to war.

What, in fact, were Hitler's long-term war plans? When did he think that his land and sea armaments would be sufficient for a general war, once Central Europe had been subdued? "In three or four years" is what Ribbentrop told Ciano on October 28, 1938. But was Ribbentrop trying to deceive Ciano? Was the Reich Foreign Minister really unaware of the Führer Directive of October 21, which had ordered preparations for the liquidation of "the remainder of Czecho-Slovakia"? This is hardly believable. It is far more likely that Ribbentrop failed to foresee that in Paris and in London Germany's blatant violation of the Munich agreement would lead to a full-scale revival of the crisis.

Hitler was thinking on similar lines. This is shown by the "Z-Plan", the extremely ambitious programme of warship construction submitted by Grand-Admiral Raeder and approved in January 1939. This programme included the building of nine huge battleships and battle-cruisers for an expanded fleet which was intended to be ready for a war by 1948.

Hitler agreed to a deadline of 1944–45 for the surface warships and 1943 for the 249 U-boats provided for in the Z-Plan.

The new Czech President, Dr Emil Hácha, is saluted by a Czech guard of honour. Elderly, honest, and sincere, Hácha had none of the physical or mental stamina needed to stand up to Hitler's threats in March 1939.

Hácha: no match for Hitler

If Hitler's "intuition" could have told him that in nine months' time he would be at war with the two greatest naval powers in Europe, he would probably have acted very differently. As he did soon after the outbreak of war, he would have dropped the battleship-building section of the Z-Plan in favour of the U-boat schedule. But when he approved the Z-Plan, the preparations for the final destruction of Czecho-Slovakia were already under way.

Hitler's plan followed the Clausewitz ideal: he would have liked to invade without meeting resistance from either Paris or London. This was no doubt wishful thinking, but the impression he had received from his meetings with Chamberlain and Daladier at the time of Munich had convinced him that this would be possible. As far as Czecho-Slovakia was concerned, Hitler's mind was already made up. Barely two days after the Munich agreement he had sent a secret message to Keitel at the O.K.W., asking

Walther von Brauchitsch was born in Berlin on October 4, 1881, the son of a cavalry officer. He received his education at a military academy, after which he was commissioned into the Prussian Guard in 1900. During World War I he served on the general staff. He continued his career in the Reichswehr after the war and rose to become Inspector of Artillery in 1932, the year he joined the Nazi Party after discovering that "Hitler has been sent by God to put an end to the harsh constraints of the Treaty of Versailles." He was given command of an army group in 1937, and the position of Commander-in-Chief of the Army after Fritsch in February 1938. He directed the operations in Poland, Scandinavia, and against the Low Countries and France, before being dismissed for the failure of the army before Moscow in December 1941. He was taken prisoner in 1945 and died in hospital in Hamburg on October 18, 1948 while awaiting trial.

Wilhelm Keitel was born in Helmscherode on September 22, 1882. He served as a staff officer in World War I and in the same capacity in the Reichswehr. After the fall of Blomberg and Fritsch in February 1938, Keitel was appointed to the new position of Chief of the Armed Forces High Command, the equivalent of War Minister. As such he was Hitler's military adviser, or rather the liaison officer between Hitler and the O.K.W. In fact his role was to give the stamp of professional military approval to Hitler's intuitive strategic and tactical ideas. He took part in all the major military conferences. It was also Keitel who dictated the armistice terms to the French in 1940. After the failure of the plot to assassinate Hitler on July 20, 1944, he sat on the court that condemned many of the conspirators to death. He was arrested in 1945, tried at Nuremberg and hanged on October 16, 1946 after being found guilty of planning and waging aggressive war.

how much time and military strength would be needed to break the resistance of the Czechs. On October 11 Keitel replied that it would take little time and not much effort.

In Czecho-Slovakia, Beneš had resigned as President on October 5, and it was not until November 30 that the Czech National Assembly found a permanent successor in Dr. Emil Hácha. Hencke, German *chargé d'affaires* in Prague, had this to say about Hácha in his report to Ribbentrop on December 2: "Until now, very little has been heard of Dr. Hácha. He has hardly enjoyed anything in the way of popularity. The new President is 66 years old. The strongest argument in his favour is that he is one of the few men in this country about whom it is impossible to say anything but good. His previous career as a judge has been impeccable, and one is struck by his integrity and by his judgement in all aspects of human and judicial affairs. He has never involved himself in politics and knows nothing about it, as he is the first to admit." Hencke added that Hácha had stated "that his country and his people can only survive if, despite all the psychological obstacles, a new relationship based on genuine mutual confidence without compromise" were established with Germany.

Without waiting for the outcome of the Czech Parliamentary elections, the Czech Foreign Minister, Chvalkovský, had been trying to head the foreign policy of his unfortunate country in this direction.

The results were not auspicious. Following the provisions of the Munich agreement, Chvalkovský had been forced to comply with every last territorial demand made by Berlin. As a result, together with the Sudeten Germans some 800,000 Czechs had passed under German rule without the least guarantee of their cultural autonomy. On the other hand, the 478,000-odd Germans who remained behind Czecho-Slovakia's new frontiers had received the privileged status of *Volksdeutsche*, which in many ways shielded them from Czech authority.

New pressure on Prague

On November 19, 1938, two protocols were signed in Berlin by the newly-appointed German Ambassador in Prague, Ritter, for Germany, and by General Husárek for Czecho-Slovakia.

"It was no longer a question of days, but of hours . . . if Slovakia wanted her independence he would support her efforts and stand surety for her success". He would only intervene from now on if German interests were threatened, which would never be the case east of the Carpathians. Germany, Hitler finished by declaring, had no interest in Slovakia, a country which historically had never formed part of Germany.

Asked for the most recent developments of the situation, Ribbentrop put an edge on Hitler's proposals by stressing that Tiso would only have a few hours in which to make his decision. A dispatch had just reached him, he said, which told of Hungarian troop movements towards the Slovak frontier.

But the Slovak ministers were not told that these troop movements, which were in fact aimed at Sub-Carpathian Ruthenia, had been organised by the Germans. Sent to Budapest on Ribbentrop's orders, Councillor Altenburg had put the idea to Admiral Miklós Horthy, Regent of Hungary, on the morning of March 13. By 1725 hours the same day, Berlin had been informed that it had been received "with enthusiasm". In fact, the lack of training in the Hungarian Army had forced the Hungarian Chief-of-Staff, who had been present at the audience with Horthy, to ask that the operation be postponed until the following week, but Altenburg had promptly retorted that this would be too late. And so Hitler was sent the following schedule by Horthy: Thursday, March 16–"frontier incident"; Saturday, March 18–"military coup".

It was in this explosive atmosphere that on the following day, March 14, the Bratislava Diet yielded to its fears of Hungarian aggression and proclaimed the independence of Slovakia. Hitler was asked "to guarantee the existence of the new state, and to take every measure to assure the protection of its frontiers". Cut off from Prague by Slovakia's secession, Sub-Carpathian Ruthenia considered itself obliged to follow Bratislava's example and its new President, Monsignor Vološín, also asked for Hitler's guarantee. But already six Hungarian brigades were advancing up the valleys towards the peaks of the Carpathians and the Polish frontier. In this situation, Berlin sent a categorical "no" to the Ruthenian President at 1700 hours on March 15, together with the advice to drop any ideas of resistance.

President Hácha's agony

The Republic of Czecho-Slovakia was no more. Slovakia had adopted Hitler's patronage. Sub-Carpathian Ruthenia had been marked down to Hungary. Bohemia and Moravia, the Czech lands, stood alone–and now it fell to President Hácha, despite his chronic heart trouble, to shoulder the agonising burden of the last frightful hours which lay ahead.

At last, the final blow fell on Czecho-Slovakia. At 1100 hours on Wednesday,

▽ *Britain's casual reaction to the knowledge that preparations must be taken to fight Germany if necessary. Even the idea is not new–it echoes the " 'Arf a mo', Kaiser" slogan of World War I. However, once the decision to reintroduce compulsory service in Britain was taken after the Prague coup, there was no wavering on the part of the government.*

March 15, Hácha and Chvalkovský arrived at the New Chancellery in Berlin. There they found, gathered around Hitler, Ribbentrop, Meissner, Weizsäcker, Dietrich, and – significantly – Göring and Keitel. Hácha and Chvalkovský were led to a room where they faced Hitler, Ribbentrop, and Göring. On the table lay a document which contained the total abdication of Czecho-Slovakia's sovereignty. "This is no time for negotiation," declared Hitler. "It is time to take note of the irrevocable decisions of the German Government." With that Hitler signed the document and stalked out of the room.

It was 0130 hours. The order had gone out for the German troops to commence the occupation of Bohemia and Moravia at 0630 hours. Five hours in which to yield! All through the night Hácha protested against this brutality and strove desperately to avoid signing his country's death-warrant. He argued that he must obtain the consent of his ministers. A telephone link to Prague was arranged. Meanwhile the German ministers pushed the two men around the table, constantly waving the papers under their noses, thrusting pens into their hands, threatening that in two hours half the city of Prague could be destroyed by 800 bombers which were only waiting for the order to take off. During this long and terrible night, Hácha had to be brought round several times by doctors standing by in the next room. At about 0345 he lost consciousness entirely and had to be given injections. From this moment his resistance was broken and he signed in desperation, convinced that if he did not he would expose his country to a pitiless bombardment.

Such was the most dramatic moment in this crisis, which historians have since called "the rape of Prague".

The paper signed by Hácha implied that the Czechs would be left some shreds of independence, or rather autonomy, by the Third Reich. But it made little difference: nothing mattered now but the advance of the Wehrmacht, which had commenced the occupation of the Czech lands and the neutralisation of the Czech Army at 0600 hours that morning. Against every Czech battalion a German division was advancing. Any resistance would be useless; it could only have resulted in futile bloodshed which would have given Hitler all the excuse he needed to deny the Czechs any vestige of autonomy. This was why Hácha had been summoned to Berlin, in the hope that he would order his troops to surrender to the Germans, and that he would do it with no questions asked.

Pushed to the final limits of their endurance, the two Czech statesmen had no alternative but to yield. They accepted the conditions laid down in the O.K.W. note of March 11, and put their names to a joint declaration which read as follows: "Berlin, March 15, 1939.

At their request, the Führer has today received President Hácha and Foreign Minister Chvalkovský in the presence of Reich Foreign Minister von Ribbentrop. At this meeting the grave situation created by the events of recent weeks in the present Czecho-Slovak territory was examined with complete frankness.

"Both sides unanimously expressed the conviction that every effort must be made to preserve calm, order, and peace in this part of Central Europe. The Czecho-Slovak President declared that, in order to pursue this object and to achieve complete pacification, he confidently placed the fate of the Czech people and country in the hands of the Führer and the German Reich. The Führer accepted this declaration and expressed his intention of taking the Czech people under the

▽ The agony begins: Dr Hácha comes to the New Chancellery to have his country's death-warrant read to him early in the morning of March 15.
▷ Hitler's triumph – "Greater Germany", with every stage in its development proudly marked. The quote from Hitler's Mein Kampf *exhorts no German to consider the Reich secure until it can offer every member of the German race his own plot of ground.*

GROSSDEUTSCHLAND

Haltet das Reich nie für gesichert, wenn
es nicht auf Jahrhunderte hinaus jedem
Sprossen unseres Volkes sein eigenes
Stück Grund und Boden zu geben vermag!

Adolf Hitler („Mein Kampf")

△ *Prague's new master, depicted on a postage stamp issued in the German "Protectorate" of Bohemia and Moravia—the Czech homelands. For these occupied territories, six years of Nazi rule lay ahead.*

▷ *The triumph of the victors: Hitler and his generals take the salute as the German Army rolls into Prague.*
▽ *Wenceslas Square echoes to the roar of a full motorised division on the move. Resistance would have been futile; it was a chilling argument in favour of the big battalions.*

protection of the German Reich, and of guaranteeing them an autonomous development of their ethnic life as suited to their character.

In token of which the present document has been signed by both parties."

Rudolf Beran, the Czech Prime Minister, and General Jan Syrový, Minister for National Defence, gave in without being pushed about or given injections. This was certainly not surprising in the case of Beran: to the question of whether or not it would be better to capitulate or to stand up to the Reich with the aid of the Red Army, Beran replied, brandishing his wallet: "Hitler will not take this from me. With Voroshilov I am not so sure . . . That is why I would rather be swallowed by Hitler than saved by Voroshilov."

New muscles for the Wehrmacht

With this document Hitler had got everything he wanted, and German troops proceeded to occupy the whole of Bohemia and Moravia as effortlessly as though they were on manoeuvres. But photographs of the event clearly show the feelings of humiliation, grief, and anger with which the Czechs greeted their oppressors. They had lost – but now the threat of a general war was imminent.

The Czech Army was disbanded but many of its officers reached the West and took up arms again a few months later, first under the French and then under the British. The Czech Army's equipment, which was abundant and relatively modern, was eagerly taken over by the Wehrmacht – especially the excellent Škoda tanks. Some 336 T-35 and T-38 tanks were used to equip the newly-formed 6th, 7th, and 8th Panzer Divisions during the "Phoney War" of 1939–40, units which would play a key rôle in the German offensives in the summer of 1940.

As might have been expected, the Germans went through the Czech Army archives in minute detail. They found much of importance. In the files of the Czech Military Intelligence department they found a report on the most recent French fortifications in north-east France. Illustrated with sketches, this document had been drawn up by a team of highly-skilled officers who had visited a sector of the Maginot Line a few years before. Its information added considerably to the data gathered by the Germans from their inspection of the Czech fortifications in the Sudetenland which had fallen into their hands after Munich.

In the field of military hardware, the important Škoda works at Pilsen were soon making an important contribution to German military preparations and to the war effort of the Third Reich. Moreover, the Škoda works had been the main source of supply for the weapons of the Rumanian and Yugoslav Armies. The Prague coup would thus prove of considerable help to Berlin in stepping up the pressure on Yugoslavia and Rumania when the time came.

◁ ◁ *The pathetic figure of Dr Hácha, flanked by jubilant German officers.* ◁ *Grief and rage distort the faces of the citizens of Prague as the Germans drive in.* △ *March 16, 1939– and Hitler arrives in the second capital to fall to him.*

△ The Reichstag rises to salute its Führer. By the spring of 1939 Hitler's policies had made Germany supreme in central Europe. The humiliation of the Versailles diktat had been wiped out. But this was not enough. Hitler was already laying his plans for the destruction of his next victim.

Czechoslovakia's epitaph

What conclusions can be drawn from this sorry business?

1. The subjection of Czechoslovakia had always been planned as being complementary to Germany's annexation of Austria. Thus to defend Prague it would have been necessary to defend Vienna. But Prague herself, despite the most obvious strategic requirements, had not a single friendly neighbouring ally except Rumania.
2. The country was not a united one. All attempts to reconcile nationalist minorities within Czechoslovakia since 1920 were insufficient to prevent Nazi Germany from exploiting their various quarrels with the Prague Government to Germany's advantage. Nor was Germany alone to blame: Slovakia only seceded in March 1939 because of the threat of Hungary. Prague's grant of autonomous government to Bratislava had come too late to give the Czechs and Slovaks a common cause.

Such were the shortcomings of the Republic of Czechoslovakia – but obvious and regrettable though they were, they were nothing to the cynical and brutal aggression of Germany which culminated in the Prague coup of March 15, 1939. It was a straight comparison between dereliction of duty and shameless crime.

CHAPTER 3
Pressure on Poland

◁ *German propaganda poster shows East Prussia severed from the Reich by the Polish Corridor.*
▽ *Józef Lipski, Polish Ambassador to Berlin, who stood up to the new claims of Hitler and Ribbentrop and refused to be intimidated.*

After Munich, Hitler was planning not only the final liquidation of Czecho-Slovakia but also his next big expansionist move. This time his victim was to be Poland.

On October 24, 1938, Ribbentrop was lunching at the Grand Hotel in Berchtesgaden with Józef Lipski, Polish Ambassador to Berlin. Between the dessert and the cheese, Ribbentrop suddenly presented his plan for a "joint solution" to all possible German-Polish differences. Warsaw should consent to the restoration of the Free City of Danzig to the Reich, to the building of an *autobahn* and railway, both extra-territorial, across the famous "Danzig Corridor" in Polish Pomerania,

and to joining the Anti-Comintern Pact. In return Berlin would guarantee Poland's economic rights and railway access to Danzig, extend the 1934 German-Polish Non-Aggression Pact, originally scheduled to run for ten years, by 25 years, and guarantee Poland's frontiers.

Ribbentrop was no more liked in Poland than he was in France. According to Count Jan Szembek, Polish Under-Secretary for Foreign Affairs, Lipski considered Ribbentrop "a most disagreeable partner who does not understand the Danzig problem, but merely keeps on repeating that Danzig is a German city. By contrast, Göring has shown that he knows full well that Danzig, if incorporated into the Reich and deprived

△ *The "home to the Reich" theme again. "Danzig is a German city and wants to return to Germany" proclaims the banner, as Nazi Gauleiter Forster inspects a parade of storm troopers in the city. As in the Czech Sudetenland, the Nazi Party was well organised in Danzig and was adept at creating "incidents" which were held up as alleged proof that the Polish Government was persecuting German citizens.*

of its Polish hinterland, would be more or less condemned to perish."

After warning his host that he saw absolutely no chance of the Free City returning to the Reich, Lipski hastened to inform his chief, Polish Foreign Minister Józef Beck, that Ribbentrop had sounded him out on the subject. Beck proved as quick on the uptake as Lipski. Less than a week after Ribbentrop's approach on the 24th, Beck's reply to Lipski left Warsaw. It contained a detailed statement on the subject of Danzig which Lipski was charged with explaining to the leaders of the Reich.

Danzig: the new prize

In Beck's opinion, the 1934 agreement with Germany had shown its value during the recent crisis in Europe. As far as Warsaw was concerned, it was not "a tactical and provisional expedient" but an expression of the definite wish of the two nations to remedy a situation which, after centuries

of mutual hostility, could profit neithe side. Thus it was intended to consolidat the friendly relations which the tw former enemies had established.

Beck was certainly not prepared t sacrifice the rights in Danzig given t Poland by the Treaty of Versailles for th sake of German-Polish concord. The im portance of Danzig's maritime trade, th expansion of its merchant fleet, and it industrial production made a concessio of this nature unacceptable to Poland. I any case the administration of the Fre City, instituted in 1919, in no way affecte the rights of the German population Nevertheless, not wishing to appear in transigent, Beck told Lipski to sugges another solution to Ribbentrop.

This would "substitute a bilatera German-Polish agreement for the pact o 1934. The new agreement would guarante the continued existence of the Free City o Danzig in such a way that the national an cultural way of life of the German majorit would be unimpaired, and that all existin Polish rights would be guaranteed. Despit the complications," Beck concluded in his instructions to Lipski, "the Polish Government is obliged to state that any other solution, and in particular the proposal to incorporate the Free City into the Reich, would inevitably lead to a conflict. Such an eventuality would not only lead to local trouble but could fatally obstruct the course of German-Polish understanding."

All this was logical. But as far as Hitler and Ribbentrop were concerned, the 1934 agreement was exactly what Beck had said it was not: "a tactical and provisional expedient". The future of German-Polish relations mattered far less to them than the gaining of Danzig. However, Lipski took his time in passing on Beck's instructions. Doubtless thinking that there was no harm in letting things ride, he waited until November 19 before calling at the German Foreign Ministry in the Wilhelmstrasse and giving Ribbentrop the gist of his instructions from Warsaw. According to Lipski's report to Beck the same day, Ribbentrop's attitude was "completely friendly", and Ribbentrop had given him to understand that his attitude on October 24 had been taken "on his own initiative". Lipski thought that Hitler had not approved of Ribbentrop's suggestions and that there was no need for his chief in Warsaw to alarm himself.

With certain reservations, Beck adopted Lipski's point of view. He considered that Ribbentrop was a novice diplomat and was very close not only to the Junker class but also to the aggressive German nationalists who followed a tradition of hostility to Poland and of general scorn for the states of eastern Europe. Personal ambition and the desire to score an impressive success had led Ribbentrop, Beck believed, to exceed Hitler's brief. Hitler, however, saw refusal in Poland's attitude. On November 24, he ordered the commanders of Germany's armed forces to set in motion preparations for the occupation of Danzig.

Hitler's plans for Danzig

Beck, however, was brought down to earth with a terrific jolt when, visiting Berchtesgaden on January 5, 1939, he listened to Hitler describing how he felt about the Danzig problem. His views were identical to those which Beck had believed had merely been dreamed up by the tactless Ribbentrop in an excess of zeal.

Hitler resumed the claims put forward by Ribbentrop on October 24: Danzig and the *autobahn*-railway link across the Corridor between the Reich and East Prussia. But he did so without any heat at all—no veiled threats or hints of future trouble. In particular, he gave Beck his word that no *fait accompli* would be engineered in Danzig by Germany.

Hitler stated that his attitude towards Poland had not changed in the least since the pact of 1934. "In any circumstances," he continued, "Germany would be greatly interested in the continued existence of a strongly nationalist Polish state because of what might happen in Russia. Whether Russia had a Bolshevik, Tsarist, or any other kind of régime, Germany's attitude towards Russia would always be marked by extreme caution . . . Quite apart from that, the existence of a strong Polish Army lightened Germany's load to a considerable degree. The divisions which Poland kept on her frontier with Russia spared Germany from a similar military burden." But Hitler's assurances did not cause Beck

▽ *As long as Hitler had other fish to fry, Germany's relations with Poland were good. Here the Polish Foreign Minister Colonel Beck (extreme left) poses with Hitler, Reich Foreign Minister Neurath, and Göring during a goodwill visit to Germany in 1935.*

△ *"The Danzig chess-game"–
and the threat of the mailed fist.
In fact, Danzig was only a
pretext: Hitler was planning
nothing less than the total
destruction of Poland as an
independent state.*

to consent to the required concessions. Still less did they disperse the apprehension which he felt about them. Replying, Beck said that the Danzig problem was extremely difficult and that he would certainly be unable to discuss it without bearing in mind the unanimous wishes of the Polish nation, which he could not and would not contravene.

Returning from Berchtesgaden, Beck had another meeting with Ribbentrop in Munich in which he spoke his mind. He asked Ribbentrop to repeat to Hitler, "that while he had always been optimistic as to the outcome of the discussions which he had had with the German statesmen, this was the first time he had felt at all pessimistic". Ribbentrop's reply was "that Germany did not envisage any violent solution" to the problems under discussion between Germany and Poland. After this first Polish rebuttal, Hitler took the initi-

ative again on January 9: he gave Poland to think that in return for her co-operation *vis-à-vis* Danzig, Germany would help her to realise her nationalistic ambitions.

When Ribbentrop travelled to Warsaw for the fifth anniversary of the German-Polish Non-Aggression Pact (January 26, 1939), both he and Beck held their different viewpoints about Danzig and the proposed extra-territorial routes. What is more, Beck turned down a suggestion from Ribbentrop that Poland should join Germany, Italy, and Japan in their Anti-Comintern Pact. But although there were no signs of any reconciliation of the different interests of Germany and Poland, the tone of the discussions remained courteous.

We know from a note by Frau von Ribbentrop, who went to Warsaw with her husband, that the news of a sudden change of attitude by the French Government,

ending its policy of neutrality towards Eastern Europe, reached Ribbentrop the very day he arrived in Warsaw. This caused an immediate alteration in Poland's position and the discussions were politely cut short. At a state banquet afterwards, the atmosphere was courteous but obviously reserved. Frau von Ribbentrop commented: "During the return journey my husband, for the first time, said to his colleagues: 'From now on we have only one choice of action if we want to escape from territorial encirclement, and that is to get an understanding with the Russians.' "

On the face of it, the meeting had been an uneventful one. Ribbentrop had been received by Ignacy Mościcki, President of the Polish Republic. A joint public statement had been signed by the two powers during the visit. On returning to Germany he had sent a cable of thanks to his host. At no time had Ribbentrop shown any sign of impatience or eagerness to see the territorial dispute between the two states resolved quickly. The same still applied to Hitler. In his speech of January 30, the sixth anniversary of his accession to power, Hitler made a flattering reference to the "great Marshal, the patriot-soldier Piłsudski". Referring to the German-Polish pact, he also declared: "At this moment there are almost no differences of opinion between our friendly, peaceful states about the importance of this instrument . . . Last year, we saw the friendship between Germany and Poland prove its worth as a guarantee of peace in the political life of Europe."

When Hitler spoke these encouraging words, had he already decided to use force against Poland if the "solution" offered on January 5 should be rejected? There can be no doubt that he had. But before offering Poland the choice of submission or an-

nihilation he had to avoid causing alarm in Warsaw during the weeks needed to complete the subjection of Czecho-Slovakia, duly achieved on March 15 with the Prague coup. The implications of the German takeover hit Poland like an earthquake. Admittedly, it gave Poland the common frontier with Hungary which she had wanted for years, and which a few months later would allow many Poles to escape to the West and carry on the fight against Germany from there. But the cynicism with which Hitler had broken his word; his callousness towards the principle of national self-determination, in whose name he had claimed and won the Sudetenland; his open contempt for the Slav peoples–all these provoked general indignation, and as far as the Polish Government was concerned proved that any negotiations on the lines proposed by Berlin would be futile.

Hitler takes Memel

Apart from this, the "protection" given to Slovakia by Germany caused much worry to the Polish Government and General Staff. Justified fears that the Wehrmacht would now be able to operate from Slovak territory meant that Poland would have to extend the deployment of her frontier armies along the Carpathians for at least a further 220 miles. Thus the strategic envelopment of Poland was tragically assisted by Slovakia's new rôle.

Given this situation, Ribbentrop's interview with Lipski on March 21 sounded like the first rumble of the storm to Warsaw. Ribbentrop not only resumed the German claims on Danzig and the Corridor: he insisted that the German-Polish agreement could not survive without Poland showing "a clear anti-Soviet attitude. Poland must understand that she has to choose between Germany and Russia." Worse still, two days later Beck read the newspaper announcements that after an ultimatum, Germany had recovered from Lithuania the port and hinterland of Memel, lost at Versailles in 1919. This made the Poles more sensitive than ever as far as Danzig was concerned.

Beck considered the situation to be "so tense" that he called a meeting of his principal ministers on March 24. According to the notes taken by Count Szembek, Beck justified his pessimistic outlook by the fact that "one of the two factors which

have always governed the position of our State–Germany–has lost the sense of responsibility shown up to now . . . we know the exact limit of our own interests . . . beyond that limit Poland can only announce a *non possumus*. It is very simple, we shall fight!"

On the other hand, if "the enemy" had "abandoned every moderation in thought and deed", he might change his tune if he found that he was dealing with a state which stuck to its guns–something which had never yet happened to Nazi Germany. Hitler and his colleagues knew that "[Poland's] political settlement of accounts with Germany will not be like the others".

In Berlin, Ambassador Lipski certainly noted the "marked coolness" with which Ribbentrop greeted him on March 26. According to Beck's instructions, Lipski restated the Polish point of view. Commenting on certain military measures which Warsaw had thought fit to take, Ribbentrop showed "a certain degree of apprehension" and added: "any aggression against Danzig on your part will be regarded as aggression against the Reich." With the peculiar blend of confidence and pessimism which typified him after March 24, Beck thought it advisable to match this last announcement with one of his own. On the 28th he summoned the German Ambassador, Hans von Moltke, and told him that "any attempt by the German Government to change the *status quo* in Danzig will be considered an act of aggression against Poland". Beck toned down the bluntness of this message by denying that Poland wanted to cause trouble in Danzig, and by declaring that he still wanted to know what kind of settlement to the Danzig problem could be reached by the two states.

"You want to negotiate at bayonet-point!" exclaimed the German Ambassador.

"That is your own method," replied Beck coldly.

Mussolini's victim: Albania

Hitler's takeover of Prague was followed within weeks by Mussolini's takeover of Albania. The German coup on March 15 had angered and humiliated the Duce, and it was Ciano who suggested that Italy's reputation might be restored in Albania. Ciano recorded his thoughts in his diary.

◁ *German military might parades before Hitler in 1939. Big military parades were the best possible medium for demonstrating the massive strength of the Third Reich.*
△ △ *Right from the beginning of Hitler's régime, pride in armed strength was impressed upon the German people. This poster advertises a display of heavy artillery at Ingolstadt in July 1933.* △ *A military stamp was put on every element of society in Nazi Germany–this is a "Reich Farmers' Day" poster for November 1937.*

"Germany's intervention does not destroy the Czechoslovakia of Versailles but the country set up at Munich and Vienna. What weight can be given in the future to those declarations and promises which concern us more directly? It is useless to deny that all this worries and humiliates the Italian people. It is necessary to give them satisfaction and compensation: Albania. I spoke about it to the Duce, to whom I also expressed my conviction that at this time we shall find neither local obstacles nor serious international complications in the way of our advance. He authorised me to telegraph to Jacomoni [Italian Minister to Albania], asking him to prepare local revolts, and he personally ordered the Navy to hold the second squadron ready at Taranto."

But Mussolini vacillated. He was worried about Yugoslavia: an Italian move against Albania might well encourage a separatist movement by the Croats in Yugoslavia, who, accepting German "protection" as the Slovaks had done, would permit the extension of German influence into the Balkans. It was not until March 23 that Mussolini gave Ciano instructions to go ahead with plans for a surprise move against Albania, which would improve Italy's strategic position considerably.

These plans were enshrined in an "Italo-Albanian agreement" composed of three dry articles, whose tone, Ciano commented, was "far more like a decree than an international pact". It was hardly likely to induce King Zog of Albania to sign it without losing face. Rome replied to King Zog's objections with an ultimatum at noon on April 6, and the following day the spearheads of an Italian expeditionary force, under General Alfredo Guzzoni–of four *Bersaglieri* regiments and a tank battalion–landed at several points on the Albanian coast. Resistance to this underhand attack was feeble and sporadic. On April 8 ex-King Zog and his wife (who had given birth to a son three days before) fled to Greece.

King Victor Emmanuel III formally assumed the Crown of Albania on April 16, adding it to those of Italy and Ethiopia. In his opinion, the game was not worth the candle . . .

France and Britain: kept in the dark

While Hitler and Ribbentrop were completing their preparations for breaking their word and swallowing the rest of Czecho-Slovakia, the politicians in Paris and London would have been extremely surprised if anyone had predicted that a general conflict would shortly arise out of Germany's and Poland's failure to reach agreement over Danzig.

In his memoirs, Georges Bonnet describes the astonishment he felt when he discovered the extent to which Beck had kept him in the dark over Poland's discussions with the Third Reich. "Why did Beck keep his opinions from the French Ambassador, his ally?" Bonnet asked Daladier later. "Did he not dare to admit to himself and to others the failure of his policy? Did he wish to keep France in the dark in order to add credibility to the efforts of his propagandists in Paris, who were eventually trying to convince us that France had more to gain than Poland in maintaining the alliance? Or did he really think that he could settle the Danzig Corridor business himself, talking with Germany as an equal?"

When Bonnet wrote his memoirs (1946–47) he did not know of the relevant documents for the period from the German Foreign Office archives. These indicate that Beck did believe that Poland could settle the Danzig problem herself. Beck clung to Hitler's statement that Germany, in view of the menace of Russia, needed the continued existence of a "strongly nationalist Polish state". Be that as it may, there is no denying that Beck's refusal to communicate fully with Britain and France meant that those powers continued to be more preoccupied with the likelihood of war in the Mediterranean than in Poland.

Many historians, writing before 1939, had argued that it was the failure of Great Britain in the years before 1914 to convince Germany that Britain would fight in aid of France, with or without a violation of Belgian territory, which resulted in the outbreak of war in the West. It was this argument which caused both France and Britain–France on January 6, 1939, and Britain on February 6–to proclaim to the world that in the event of a war they would co-operate. In his speech to the House of Commons, Chamberlain added: "Any threat to the vital interests of France, from wherever it might come, will necessarily provoke the immediate involvement of our country."

So it was that Mussolini, at the moment when he was doubling the strength of the Italian Army in Libya and insulting France with a mud-slinging press campaign, suddenly realised that any Italian attempt to take over Tunis would automatically bring the British Fleet against him.

France and Britain, however, were brought rudely to their senses when Hitler's troops marched into Bohemia and Moravia on March 15. The Prague coup produced an immediate and indignant protest from both countries. In a note dated March 17, France condemned the "flagrant violation of both the letter and the intent" of the Munich agreement, declaring that "the circumstances in which the leaders of the Republic of Czechoslovakia were forced to submit on March 15 have no foundation in right . . ." and concluded: "The Government of the Republic, under these circumstances, does not recognise the validity of the new situation created in Czechoslovakia by the action of the Reich." The British Ambassador in Berlin, Sir Nevile Henderson, handed over a similar note.

On March 31 the funeral speech of appeasement was pronounced when Neville Chamberlain rose in the House of Commons and announced Britain's guarantee of immediate military aid in the event of any threat to Poland's independence. France had no need to make a similar declaration: her aid had already been pledged in the Franco-Polish military

◁ Mussolini strikes east: Bersaglieri *wheel their bicycles ashore in Albania on April 6, 1939. The feeble régime of King Zog* (inset) *collapsed at once, and Albania became a province of the Italian Empire.*
▽ "The King-Emperor and the Founder of the Empire". King Victor Emmanuel regarded the glittering titles heaped upon him by Mussolini with a considerable amount of cynicism.

IL RE IMPERATORE E IL FONDATORE DELL'IMPERO

treaty of 1921, which had never lapsed. The result of the Italian takeover of Albania in the following week was two more guarantees on April 13, from France as well as from Britain, to Rumania and Greece.

Chamberlain, then, had pledged his country to fight against the future ambitions of the Axis—but the French were quick to point out that Britain lacked the military wherewithal to do so. Conscription was the stumbling-block. To France it was ludicrous that Britain should rely on her paperweight Regular Army to enforce such solemn guarantees of military aid to foreign powers. In Britain, however, the Labour Opposition took more persuading. After the war the Labour Party in the House of Commons was the first to put the blame for World War II on "Tory mismanagement" in the years before 1939. But it had been the Labour M.P.s who had voted down pleas for British rearmament in the 1930's with vicious attacks on "Tory armaments", and who in early 1939 championed the fight against the reintroduction of conscription in Britain. Yet there was no stopping Chamberlain now: his mind was made up.

The vote for conscription was cast on April 27, and it was passed by 380 votes to 143. It was, of course, far too late for Britain to produce a sizeable and battleworthy conscript army for service in 1939. Yet the symbolic value of the reintroduction of

"Not only have I united the German people politically, but I have also rearmed them. I have also endeavoured to destroy, sheet by sheet, that treaty which in its 448 articles contains the vilest oppression which peoples and human beings have ever been expected to endure."

conscription was not lost.

Especially not on Adolf Hitler. He reacted promptly in a speech in the Reichstag on the following day, April 28. American correspondent William Shirer, who witnesses the event, recorded his feelings in his *Berlin Diary:*
"Berlin, April 28.
Hitler in the Reichstag today denounced a couple more treaties . . . loudly applauded by the rubber-stamp 'parliamentarians'. Hitler denounces the naval accord with Britain [signed in June 1935, giving Ger-

many the right to build up a navy of 35% of the strength of the Royal Navy] on the grounds that London's 'encirclement policy' has put it out of force–a flimsy excuse; of course no excuse at all. The second treaty denounced, the 1934 pact with Poland, is more serious, the excuse, incidentally, being the same . . .

"Still much doubt here among the informed whether Hitler has made up his mind to begin a world war for the sake of Danzig. My guess is he hopes to get it by the Munich method."

◁ △ *Göring in conversation with Sir Nevile Henderson, British Ambassador in Berlin.*
◁ *Young Danzigers proclaim their pro-Nazi sympathies in a carefully posed alfresco rally.*
△ *Hitler in full flood during his impassioned speech in the Reichstag on April 28, 1939. In this speech he denounced Britain's anti-German policy, the Anglo-German naval agreement of 1935, and–most significant of all–the non-aggression pact which had bound Poland and Germany since 1934.*

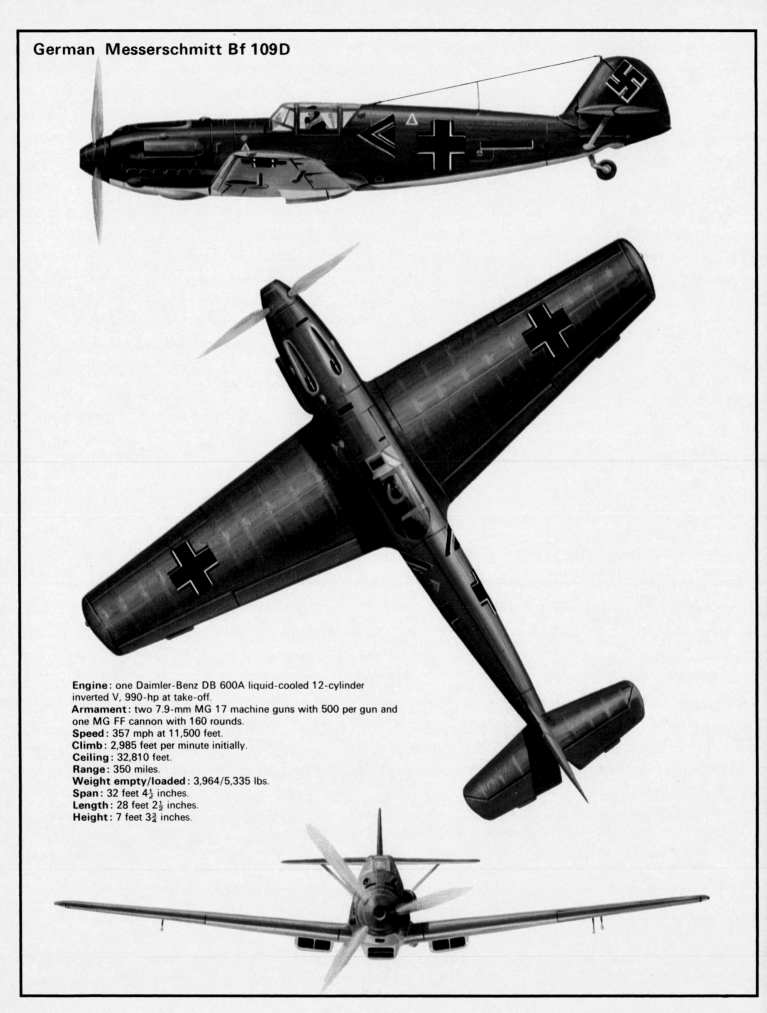

German Messerschmitt Bf 109D

Engine: one Daimler-Benz DB 600A liquid-cooled 12-cylinder inverted V, 990-hp at take-off.
Armament: two 7.9-mm MG 17 machine guns with 500 per gun and one MG FF cannon with 160 rounds.
Speed: 357 mph at 11,500 feet.
Climb: 2,985 feet per minute initially.
Ceiling: 32,810 feet.
Range: 350 miles.
Weight empty/loaded: 3,964/5,335 lbs.
Span: 32 feet $4\frac{1}{2}$ inches.
Length: 28 feet $2\frac{1}{2}$ inches.
Height: 7 feet $3\frac{3}{4}$ inches.

THE AXIS ARSENAL: a one-sided story

◁ The Messerschmitt Bf 109D was Germany's standard fighter in 1938, and was the result of the lessons learnt with the 109C during the Spanish Civil War. Engine power was increased 20 per cent, and cannon armament was fitted for the first time. The 109D was a good gun platform and handled well, especially in roll, but had poor ground characteristics because of its narrow-track undercarriage and inadequate visibility. 235 were still in service in September 1939.

▽ The strongest German surface ships in service in 1939 were the battle-cruisers Scharnhorst (below) and her sister ship the Gneisenau. Their 11-inch gun main armament was lighter than that of their British counterparts (Hood, Repulse, and Renown all had 15-inch guns) but their armour protection was much greater. They were, in effect, small battleships.

When the Pact of Steel was signed in May 1939, there was considerable jubilation on the Italian side. To a certain extent, this was shared by their political opposite numbers on the German side. But not so the military–the German High Command had good reason to doubt the martial efficiency of their newly-acquired allies, the Italian armed forces.

By 1939 the Wehrmacht had evolved an armoured force which was second to none. Admittedly, its tanks were in some ways inferior to contemporary French and British vehicles, but in numbers, organisation, and tactical thinking, the Panzer forces held a considerable, indeed commanding, lead.

The Luftwaffe was equipped with fast, efficient medium and dive-bombers, protected by high-performance monoplane fighters, and supported by good communications, excellent anti-aircraft defences, and an imaginative offensive doctrine.

The Italian armed forces possessed neither of these advantages. Italian tank theory and design were both primitive, obsolete, and unimaginative. In fact, the Italian armoured forces suffered from the Allied disease of considering the tank as an adjunct of the infantry, rather than a weapon in its own right.

As far as the Italian Air Force was concerned, matters were slightly better. The Italians did,

in fact, possess bombers that were a match for their German equivalents. But the logistical backing and tactical doctrine with which they were intended to operate was in the one case hopelessly inadequate, and in the other entirely outmoded. As far as aerial protection was concerned, the Italian Air Force was still effectively in the biplane era.

And this is only one field in which the disparity between the German and Italian armed forces may be compared. In addition to this, Italy's army was hopelessly weak in anti-tank and anti-aircraft guns, her artillery was under-strength and out of date, and the standard of Italian automatic weapons–light and heavy

Displacement: 32,000 tons.
Armament: nine 11-inch, twelve 5.9-inch, fourteen 4.1-inch, sixteen 37-mm A.A., ten 20-mm A.A., six 21-inch torpedo tubes, and four aircraft.
Armour: 13-inch belt, 12-inch turrets, and 6-inch deck.
Speed: 31½ knots.
Radius: 10,000 miles at 19 knots.
Complement: 1,800.

41

Czech TNHP

Weight: 11 tons.
Crew: 4.
Armament: one 37-mm gun with 90 rounds and two 7.9-mm machine guns with 2,700 rounds.
Armour: 15-mm minimum, 50-mm maximum.
Engine: Praga EPA/O, 125-hp.
Speed: 35 mph maximum.
Range: 125 miles.
Length: 15 feet 2 inches.
Width: 6 feet 9 inches.
Height: 7 feet 11 inches.

Italian L 3-35

Weight: 3½ tons.
Crew: 2.
Armament: two 8-mm FIAT Model 14/35 machine guns with 3,200 rounds.
Armour: hull nose, belly, and superstructure front and mantel 13.5-mm; hull sides, glacis plate, and superstructure sides and rear 8.5-mm; rest 6-mm.
Engine: SPA CV 3, 43-hp.
Speed: 26 mph maximum.
Range: 62 miles maximum.
Length: 10 feet 4¾ inches.
Width: 4 feet.
Height: 4 feet 2¾ inches.

△ *The Czech TNHP medium tank was the result of continuous development of a light tank introduced by the Českomoravská Kolben Daněk company in 1933. The design had been updated and fitted with improved armour and armament until it became the TNHP of 1938. In German service it was further up-armoured and used as the chassis for a family of self-propelled weapons.* △▷ *The Italian L 3-35 had its origins in the CV 33 tankette, based on the British Carden Lloyd, first built in 1933.*

machine guns – was very poor.

Only at sea could Italy make a genuine contribution to the Axis war machine. Germany had had to rebuild her navy from scratch after her World War I battle fleet had been scuttled by its own crews in Scapa Flow in 1919, and by 1939 the heaviest German capital ships in service were the battle-cruisers *Scharnhorst* and *Gneisenau*. In the field in which Germany had excelled in World War I, submarine warfare, the position was hardly better. The

designs of the boats were entirely adequate, and building capacity was expanding fairly rapidly, but the emphasis placed on heavy warship construction had held back the submarine programme to the extent that a large-scale submarine campaign against Allied shipping was out of the question.

The Italian World War I Dreadnoughts, on the other hand, had been extensively rebuilt and modernised, and a new squadron of up-to-date battleships was in

the process of completion. In addition to this formidable battle fleet, Italy also had a strong and enterprising submarine arm. And finally, her coastal forces, building on the experience of World War I, were among the best in Europe. But even this useful Italian fleet had its limitations: the country's depressingly low stocks of oil fuel.

Both the Germans and the Italians had had the invaluable experience of the Spanish Civil War in which to test their new

Weight: 9.8 tons.
Crew: 3.
Armament: one 2-cm KwK 38 gun with 180 rounds and one 7.9-mm MG 34 with 1,425 rounds.
Armour: hull front 35-mm, sides 20-mm; turret front 30-mm, sides 15-mm; belly 5-mm; decking 15-mm.
Engine: Maybach HL 62 TR, 140-hp.
Speed: 25 mph maximum.
Range: 118 miles maximum.
Length: 15 feet 9¼ inches.
Width: 7 feet 5¾ inches.
Height: 6 feet 7½ inches.

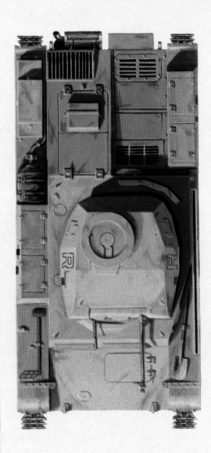

weapons under actual combat conditions, and thus iron out the seething troubles that could spell disaster in a conflict involving either of the two countries directly. The German armed forces had benefited from the opportunities thus offered; the Italians had not. Both had indeed utilised the chance to test the weapons then in service, but whereas this had been only a starting point for the Germans, the Italians had seen it as an end in itself. Germany's leaders had realised that any

future war involving their country would be fought on a larger scale and against superior opponents. Therefore they had devoted much thought to the lessons of the Civil War, with a view to amassing practical experience on which to base improvements in existing weapons and the design of the next generation of tanks and aircraft, as well as the formulation of better tactical doctrines.

The Italians, on the other hand, were satisfied with their success in the Spanish Civil War, and

assumed that they could win any future war with the same weapons and the same tactical ideas.

This was also partially the result of the widely differing standards of professionalism in the two countries. At the highest levels Italy never produced a Guderian to transform the armoured strength of the army, nor a Milch to create and organise a modern air force. At the lower levels, the Italian Army had never had the necessity for a forcing ground such as the Reichswehr

△ *The German Pzkw II light tank formed, with the Pzkw I, the backbone of the German Panzer forces until well after the beginning of the war. It was designed originally as a stop-gap training tank pending the arrival of the Pzkw III and IV, the next generation of German tanks. But delays in the production programme of these heavier vehicles meant that the Pzkw II had to be pressed into front line service, in which it performed very creditably until the Russian campaign of 1941.*

had been, and this, combined with emphasis being placed on political enthusiasm rather than professional competence, meant that the Italian officer corps was incapable of providing good leadership. The training and morale of the rank and file was, consequently, at a very low ebb.

Thus there was a complete contrast between the armed forces of the Axis partners. What about the industrial backing that would be required for a major war? Here again there was no real comparison. Italian factories were not capable of producing anything like the quantity, or the quality, of war matériel that could be supplied by Germany's massive industrial centres. And after the takeover of Czechoslovakia in March 1939, Germany's lead was increased still further, for the weapons then placed at her disposal – in particular the Czech tanks – were of an extremely high standard. The Škoda armament factories also became an important supply centre for the Cerman Army.

In addition to the widely differing industrial capacities of the two partners to produce armaments, there was also an enormous disparity in the raw materials available to each. Although Germany was dependent on import for supply of a few essentials, particularly the petroleum products, she could support a fairly lengthy war with the stockpiles she had built up. Italy, however, had stockpiled virtually no war essentials, had very few raw materials available to her in Italy or in her empire, and was fatally dependent on imports. She even lacked the coal with which to work iron and provide power for other vital industries.

The obvious imbalance between the Axis partners is reflected in the hardware illustrated here: the German Messerschmitt Bf 109D-1 single-seat fighter, the Pzkw (for *Panzerkampfwagen* or "armoured battle vehicle") II light tank, and the Czech TNHP medium tank, which was taken into the

Panzer forces as the Pzkw 38(t).

The Italian armed forces are represented by the FIAT C.R. 32 biplane fighter and the L 3-35 light tank (or rather machine gun carrier) which is here shown in its flamethrower form with the projector, capable of firing its flame up to 100 yards, replacing the two machine guns of the standard version. As a flame-thrower, the L 3-35 usually towed a wheeled tank containing 1,100 pounds of flame fuel. The ordinary version, though a good vehicle in its day, was now obsolete, but still served in considerable numbers with the Italian Army.

These, then, were the armed forces of Italy and Germany when the Pact of Steel was signed. Four months later, Germany was to launch World War II with her forces. Italy was to enter the war ten months after that, with her army and air force little improved from that discussed here. Even the lessons of the first few months of the war were to fail to sink into Italy's complacency.

▷ *The FIAT C.R. 32 was obsolete in 1938, but formed the backbone of the Italian fighter forces. It had proved a great success in the first part of the Spanish Civil War, but the arrival of modern Russian aircraft had proved its drawbacks. Its delightful manoeuvrability had endeared it to Italian pilots, however, and they were unwilling to move with the times into fighters with heavier armament, enclosed cockpits, armour protection, and retractable undercarriages.*

▽ *Italy had no modern battleships in service in 1939. Ships like* Conte de Cavour *made up her battle fleet. But the* Cavour, *originally a World War I Dreadnought, had been radically overhauled between 1933-37 and transformed into a much more formidable warship. Other reconstructed battleships serving in 1939 were* Giulio Cesare, Andrea Doria, *and* Caio Duilio.

Displacement: 29,000 tons.
Armament: ten 12.6-inch, twelve 4.7-inch, eight 3.9-inch A.A., eight 37-mm A.A., twelve 20-mm A.A.
Armour: 10-inch belt, 11-inch turrets, and 5½-inch deck.
Speed: 26 knots.
Complement: 1,236. (Compare with *Scharnhorst*, p.41).

Italian Fiat C.R.32

Engine: one FIAT A.30 R.A.bis liquid-cooled 12-cylinder inverted V, 600-hp at take-off.
Armament: two 12.7mm Breda-SAFAT machine guns with 375 rounds each, plus twelve $4\frac{1}{2}$-lb anti-personnel bombs.
Speed: 221 mph at 9,840 feet.
Climb: 10 minutes to 16,400 feet.
Ceiling: 25,750 feet.
Range: 485 miles.
Weight empty/loaded: 3,205/4,220 lbs.
Span: 31 feet 2 inches.
Length: 24 feet $5\frac{3}{8}$ inches.
Height: 8 feet 11 inches.

CHAPTER 4
The Pact of Steel

This, then, was the background to the gradual Italo-German *rapprochement* which culminated, on May 22, 1939, in the signing of the "Pact of Steel".

On November 6, 1937, Italy had joined the Anti-Comintern Pact, which had bound Germany and Japan since November 25 of the previous year. This diplomatic line-up was not, in fact, an alliance in the full sense of the word. It did not even recognise the Soviet Union as a state, but was intended to counter the subversive activity allegedly organised all over the world by the Comintern, from Moscow. This was why Article 1 of the Anti-Comintern Pact stated: "The contracting powers undertake to inform each other of the activity of the International Communist Party, to consult each other on measures of defence and to execute these measures of defence in direct collaboration."

Mussolini had not joined the Pact because of fears for his own Fascist régime in

Italy: he wished rather to end the isolation into which his ventures in Ethiopia and in Spain had led Italy. The day after the signing of the Anti-Comintern Pact, Ciano noted in his diary: "After signing the Pact we went to the Duce's residence. I have rarely seen him so happy. The situation of 1935 is no more. Italy has broken through her isolation: she is at the centre of the most formidable military and political system which has ever existed."

Perhaps, wrote Ciano, the common road which the three powers were now treading would even lead them to battle, to the "necessary battle" which must be fought to break the restrictions on the energies and aspirations of young nations. Nevertheless the Anti-Comintern Pact, like the old Triple Alliance of 1882 between Berlin, Rome, and Vienna, was basically nothing more than what Bismarck once called a "treaty of accord".

Had Baron von Neurath, still Reich Foreign Minister at the time, been thinking of a more direct relationship between Germany and Italy? Or had he accepted the advice which his Ambassador in Rome, Ulrich von Hassell, had given him (to the fury of Ciano and Mussolini): not to put any trust in Italy's military and economic strength? There is no way of knowing. In any case, Neurath was replaced in February 1938 by Ribbentrop, one of whose first acts was to dismiss Hassell in disgrace. Hassell's replacement was Hans Georg von Mackensen, a man with far more sympathy towards the totalitarian régimes of the Führer and the Duce.

Ribbentrop's anglophobia caused Ciano to write "Very good!" in his diary when he heard that Ribbentrop had taken over as Reich Foreign Minister. But many different factors prevented the formation of a direct alliance between Germany and Italy until May 1939.

First came the Austrian *Anschluss* in March 1938. Mussolini was not unwilling to see Austria absorbed by the Third Reich, but he and his advisers did have doubts about the reactions which such an annexation would provoke south of the Brenner Pass, among the pro-German population of the region which the Italians call the Alto Adige and the Austrians the South Tyrol. Then, on April 16, 1938, the signature

▽ *November 25, 1936: the Anti-Comintern Pact is formed. Count Kimitomo, seated on Ribbentrop's right, signs for Japan.*

▷ *The Führer and the Duce: the two dictators present a united front during Hitler's visit to Italy (May 3–9, 1939). Mussolini gave invaluable aid to Hitler by backing Germany's expansionist claims; but what Italy had to offer–or gain–as a military ally of Germany had yet to be seen.*

of the Anglo-Italian Protocol, settling the two countries' differences arising from the war in Abyssinia, made Ciano shelve the idea of an alliance with Germany. And finally there was a personality problem: Ribbentrop. He seemed completely unable to inspire any sympathy or confidence.

When Hitler and Ribbentrop visited Italy between May 3–9, 1938, the "exuberance" of the new Reich Foreign Minister disturbed Ciano greatly. On May 6 Ciano noted: "The Duce says that [Ribbentrop] is one of those Germans who mean only trouble for Germany. He speaks of war – war to the left, war to the right – without naming his enemy or defining his objectives. Sometimes he is all for joining forces with Japan and destroying Russia. At other times he wishes to hurl his thunderbolts against France and England. He has often hinted that he would like to take on the United States. All this makes me treat any ideas of his with the greatest caution."

Hitler has his doubts; no triple alliance yet

On May 12, 1938, with Franco-Italian negotiations about the Red Sea and Spain hanging fire, Mussolini told Ciano to sound out Berlin on the possibility of an alliance with Germany in which Japan would also be associated. But the negotiations were postponed on Hitler's request.

Hitler seems to have thought that the conversion of the Anti-Comintern Pact into a triple alliance at that time would have more drawbacks than advantages. In Paris and London, such a move would undermine the positions of Daladier and Chamberlain, both of whom, he knew, favoured peace. As for the United States, the inclusion of Japan in such a combination would discourage the isolationist party and make the American Government more likely to seek a closer relationship with France and Britain. Apart from these reasons the Wehrmacht had much to say on the military implications of an Italian alliance (but this was kept from Mussolini). The German military chiefs were deeply divided as to the worth of the Italian armed forces and how much of a libility they might prove. Grand-Admiral Raeder welcomed the prospect of getting help from Mussolini's navy; Colonel-Generals Keitel and Brauchitsch had many reservations about the fighting value of Italy's land forces.

Mussolini parla a Berlino: "Alla gente che ansiosa in tutto il mondo si domanda che cosa può uscire dall'incontro di Berlino, guerra o pace, il Führer ed io possiamo rispondere insieme a voce alta: la pace." *(Disegno di A. Beltrame)*

Towards a triple alliance

This resulted in a veritable cross-fire of notes, all of them friendly, but all dilatory. Agreement seemed impossible.

Immediately after the Munich conference, Ribbentrop suggested a triple alliance to Ciano, claiming that this would be "the greatest thing in the world". But Ciano did not share Ribbentrop's facile enthusiasm; he noted coldly: "I think that we will study this very carefully and then put it aside for a while."

Hitler had therefore changed his tune since May. He justified this by referring to two new factors which the Sudetenland crisis had made apparent. Before Munich the position of the French and British Governments had been so secure that even the conclusion of a triple alliance would

not have endangered them seriously. Second, on sensing the threat of war the United States had shown every sign of a desire for isolation. This feeling would only be strengthened if Japan should be involved by treaty in any new conflict provoked by Germany or Italy.

On October 28 Ribbentrop–"vain, shallow, and boastful", as Ciano later described him–visited Mussolini and Ciano and explained that war with the Western democracies must be considered inevitable within the next three or four years. But the Fascist leaders, while listening politely, managed to avoid giving a straight reply. Both Ciano and Mussolini had different– not to say completely opposing–reasons for this. On the evening of the audience, Ciano noted: "[Ribbentrop] has war on the brain. He wants war–*his* war. He has no precise plan, or at least he does not say that he has. He does not name his enemy nor define his objectives. Yet he wants war in three or four years. I was as reserved as possible, but I gave him to understand that we have many other problems which need solving, and different conceptions of the organisation and future of international life."

For his part Mussolini assured Ribbentrop that he was keen to conclude such an alliance, but that he felt the time was not yet ripe. It would be necessary beforehand to get the bulk of the Italian population enthusiastic about the scheme. He also added that Nazi Germany's anti-Catholic policies had considerably damaged the goodwill of the Italian people towards Germany. But above everything else the defensive nature of the alliance suggested by Ribbentrop did not satisfy Mussolini. There was absolutely no need, said Mussolini, for an alliance of this nature. "No one would dream of attacking the totalitarian states. We wish, for our part, to change the map of the world. To do that we need to settle objectives and conquests. We Italians already know where we must go."

Ribbentrop agreed heartily with all this, which certainly suited him better than the reserved attitude of Ciano, but the talks halted there for the time being. Two months later, Mussolini revised his attitude again. Returning to Rome for the New Year, he explained to Ciano that the current course of events no longer justified the reservations which he had expressed on October 28 as to when it would be possible to convert the Axis relationship into a military pact. The similar arrangement which existed (according to Mussolini) between Britain and France, the "bellicose" attitude of the French Government, not to mention the rearmament of the United States, evidently intended to assist the Western democracies – all these made the forming of an alliance capable of withstanding any possible coalition both necessary and urgent. In any case, the current tension between France and Italy had made the idea of an alliance with the Third Reich far more popular in Italy.

Reluctance in Tokyo

The following day Ciano wrote to Ribbentrop in this vein, for Mussolini wanted to sign the treaty in the first ten days of January. But the third member of the projected alliance – Japan – had other ideas. On September 26, 1938, Japan's Prime Minister, Prince Konoye, had dismissed General Ugaki from his post as Foreign Minister. After holding the office himself for several months, Konoye gave the Foreign Ministry to Baron Hiranuma on February 4, 1939. And this change of ministers in Tokyo put the brake on Japan's swing in favour of the Axis.

Baron Hiranuma did not reject out of hand the idea of converting the Anti-Comintern Pact into a military alliance. He had grave reservations, however, as to whether or not Japan should involve herself in the various quarrels of Italy and Germany on the other side of the world. Ambassadors Toshio Shiratori in Rome, and General Hiroshi Oshima in Berlin, both encouraged Hiranuma in his scepticism.

The result was a series of extremely delicate negotiations which took up the first three months of 1939. To cut a long story short, Japan declined to join the proposed alliance because of the Italo-German insistence on excluding France and Britain. But the Japanese formula, directed solely against the Soviet Union, was not attractive to Italy and Germany. Italy felt absolutely no threat to herself from Moscow; nor did Germany, now that details of the chaos caused in the Red Army by Stalin's purges were beginning to reach the West. Neither Germany nor Italy were at all inclined to get involved in a full-scale war over some remote incident in Japanese Manchuria or eastern Siberia.

However, negotiations between Rome and Berlin continued. On April 5–6, the

◁ October 1937: Italy's Corriere della Sera *gives front-page treatment to Mussolini's visit to Berlin and his speech stressing that he and the Führer only wanted peace. Mussolini had proclaimed the "Axis" relationship between Italy and Germany on November 1, 1936 – but two and a half years of hard bargaining were needed to convert it into a full-blown military alliance.*
▽ Italian colonial troops at drill. Mussolini had taken the German goose-step or parade-marsch, *called it the* passo Romano *("Roman step"), and imposed it on the Italian Army. The results were not always impressive and the Duce frequently raged at the Italian people's "lack of military spirit".*

German and Italian Chiefs-of-Staff Colonel-General Keitel and General Alberto Pariani, met at Innsbruck. Both agreed that war between the totalitarian powers and the Western democracies was inevitable, although it would probably not come for three or four years. But it is noteworthy that while Pariani said nothing to Keitel about Mussolini's plans to attack Albania, Keitel said nothing to Pariani about Hitler's plans to attack Poland.

Here it was already, then: the fatal pattern of "parallel war" which was to bedevil the war efforts of the two Axis powers in the years ahead, with Italy and Germany pursuing their different objectives in the Mediterranean and European theatres. But the record of the Keitel-Pariani talks reveals another inconsistency which was just as serious for the Axis.

Italy: hopelessly unready for war

When Keitel expressed doubts about the possibility of localising the Italo-French conflict which seemed likely to break out at any moment, Pariani replied grandly that if this happened all Italy would ask of her German partner would be supplies of raw materials and weapons. However, three weeks later, on April 29, Mussolini declared himself "extremely annoyed" with the woeful lack of readiness in the Italian Army and Air Force.

Such was Mussolini's anger that Ciano added some comments of his own. "The military make great play with a lot of names. They multiply the number of divisions, but in reality these are so small that they scarcely have more than the strength of regiments. The depôts are short of ammunition. Our artillery is obsolete. Our anti-aircraft and anti-tank guns are totally inadequate. There has been a good deal of bluffing in the military sphere, and even the Duce has been deceived—a tragic bluff. We will not talk about the Air Force. Valle [Air Force Chief-of-Staff and Under-Secretary of State for the Air] states that there are 3,006 first-line aircraft, while the Navy information service says that there are only 982. A gross exaggeration..." Nor were the leaders of Germany's armed forces in ignorance of this lack of Italian preparedness for war.

Returning to the subject on May 2, Ciano did not hesitate to blame Mussolini,

Komintern am Werk

(Karl Arnold)

In Spanien

„Hier herrscht in der Tat ewiger Friede! Wir wollen den Ossietzky nicht unterschätzen, aber den Friedens-Nobelpreis hätten eigentlich wir bekommen müssen."

In Frankreich

„Allons, Marianne, unsere Sowjets wollen endlich Taten sehen!"

Das Ziel

„Es ist absolut gleichgültig, ob 90 v. H. der Menschen zugrunde gehen, wenn nur die restlichen 10 v. H. zuverlässige Kommunisten sind, die die Existenz der Sowjets sicherstellen..." Lenin

Deutsch-japanische Abwehrfront „HALT!!"

riting: "But what is the Duce doing? His attention seems to be directed mostly to matters of drill: there is trouble if the present arms' is badly performed, or if an officer does not know how to do the goose-step, but he seems little concerned about the real weaknesses, of which he is certainly very well aware. In spite of my formal charges in connection with the results of the investigations by Cavagnari [Under-secretary of State and Chief-of-Staff for the Navy] into the efficiency of our Air Force he has done nothing, absolutely nothing; and today in his conversation with Cavagnari he did not mention the matter. Why? Does he fear the truth so much that he is unwilling to listen?"

But Mussolini was not so blind to the facts as Ciano feared. Without abandoning the idea of a military alliance with the Third Reich, he tried to arrange matters so that it would not come into effect as far as Italy was concerned until 1943. This was why, when Ciano was preparing to meet Ribbentrop at Lake Como on May 6, Mussolini had told him to state the following considerations:

"It is my firm belief that the two European Axis powers need a period of peace of at least three years. It will be only after 1943 that a war programme will have a really good chance of success. Italy needs such a period of peace for the following reasons:

1. To complete the military organisation of Libya and Albania, pacify Abyssinia, and to form from the latter an army of 500,000 men;
2. To build and fit out six new battleships;
3. To up-date our medium and heavy artillery;
4. To thwart, by achieving self-sufficiency, the attempts of the colonial democracies to blockade us;
5. To celebrate the 1942 Exhibition, commemorating the 20th anniversary of the Fascist Régime, which will bring in much hard currency;
6. To bring home the Italians working in France—a very serious problem from both the military and moral points of view;
7. To complete the transfer, which has already begun, of many war industries from the Po Valley to southern Italy; and
8. To strengthen the ties not only between our two governments but between our peoples. A reconciliation between the Nazi Party and the German Catholic Church, as well as the Vatican, would be of great value here.

"For all these reasons, although convinced

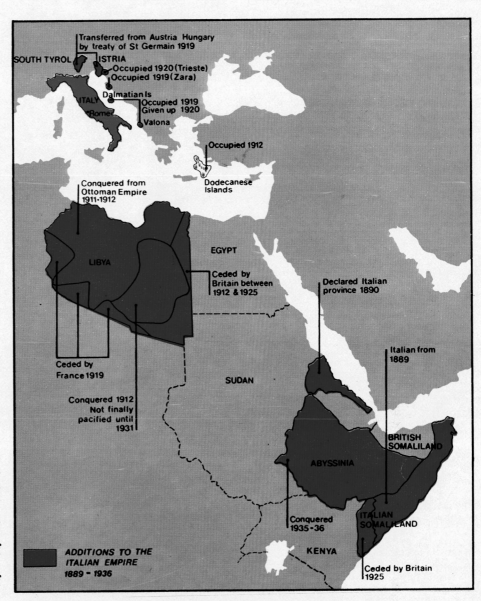

ADDITIONS TO THE ITALIAN EMPIRE 1889 – 1936

Transferred from Austria Hungary by treaty of St Germain 1919
SOUTH TYROL · ISTRIA
Occupied 1920 (Trieste)
Occupied 1919 (Zara)
Dalmatian Is
Occupied 1919 Given up 1920
ITALY · Rome
Valona
Occupied 1912
Dodecanese Islands
Conquered from Ottoman Empire 1911-1912
LIBYA
EGYPT
Ceded by Britain between 1912 & 1925
Declared Italian province 1890
Ceded by France 1919
SUDAN
Italian from 1889
Conquered 1912 Not finally pacified until 1931
BRITISH SOMALILAND
ABYSSINIA
Conquered 1935-36
ITALIAN SOMALILAND
KENYA
Ceded by Britain 1925

△ Libya, Abyssinia, Albania—the growth of the Italian Empire, which Mussolini intended to dominate North Africa and the Mediterranean. Both Britain and France were threatened by the grandiose schemes of the Duce: France in the western Mediterranean, Britain in Egypt and East Africa.
▽ Preliminary to the "Pact of Steel": Ciano and Ribbentrop meet at Milan, May 6–7, 1939.

△ *General Ugo Cavallero, Italian Chief of General Staff, takes a ceremonial "dagger salute" at a parade in Rome.*
▷ △ *Memorial service in Berlin for the men of the "Condor Legion", the German force which fought on Franco's side, killed in the Spanish Civil War.*
▷ *Triumphant parade for the survivors: Hitler takes the salute at a march-past by men of the Condor Legion. The Spanish Civil War effectively ended with the fall of Madrid on March 28, 1939. It had been an invaluable training-ground for the troops and airmen of the Wehrmacht.*

that the outcome is inevitable, Fascist Italy does not want a premature European war. It may be, too, that in three years Japan will have concluded her war in China."

In the end Ciano met Ribbentrop at Milan, not Como. As certain Parisian newspapers had hinted that Ribbentrop would not be well received in the Lombard capital, Mussolini demanded that the last conference before the signing of the alliance must be held there. During the discussions on May 6–7, Ciano was favourably impressed by the "pleasant restraint" which Ribbentrop displayed on this occasion. An agreement was reached on a military alliance between the two Axis powers, and after a telephone call from Mussolini on the evening of the 6th it was decided, after Hitler had given his consent, to announce the alliance to the press without further delay.

At this historic meeting, Ribbentrop declared his belief that peace would last for another four or five years. This, he added, would allow Germany to build up her army to full strength and to complete the construction of a fleet of heavy warships.

When Ciano got on to the subject of the German-Polish problem, Ribbentrop refused to be drawn. While remaining ready to take "the very hardest line" if Warsaw chose to try a political offensive, he could affirm that the intentions of the Reich were to let the question alone without making

any new offers, but without closing the door on negotiations.

"The programme," noted Ciano, "is not one of taking the initiative: time is on Germany's side. There are signs that people in France and Britain are getting tired of the Polish problem, and it is certain that in a few months not a Frenchman nor an Englishman will march to Poland's aid."

But was Ribbentrop genuinely unaware that on April 3, 1939, Hitler had approved *Fall Weiss* ("Case White") – the plan for the military destruction of Poland? Or had he been deliberately kept in the dark? Even today, over 30 years later, and with so many German documents available, it is difficult to give a clear yes or no.

"Real dynamite"

On May 13 Ciano read the draft of the pact for the first time. "I have never read such a pact," he noted. "It contains some real dynamite."

Ciano was right. In the preamble, the two peoples affirmed their resolution to stand shoulder to shoulder with combined forces "for the realisation [*Verwirklichung*] of their living space and the maintenance of peace". But even more serious was the fact that the reason for the alliance, described in Article 3 of the Pact, contained none of the diplomatic precautions in current use to shield either party from an obligation to aid the other if either of them resorted to unprovoked aggression.

It stated, quite clearly: "If the desires and hopes of one of the contracting powers leads it into war with another power or number of powers, the other contracting power will immediately come to its partner's aid with its full military strength, on land, on sea, and in the air." The Pact, in short, bound Italy to consider every power in the world as a possible enemy – even traditional allies such as Great Britain.

If Ciano raised no objection to Article 3, it could well have been because its wording guaranteed reciprocal aid from Germany in the event of possible Italian ventures

On the following day, seated at Hitler's right hand, Ciano signed the document which Berlin and Rome flamboyantly entitled the "Pact of Steel". Ciano would have been disenchanted, however, if he could have guessed that within 24 hours Hitler would make a mockery of the Pact by issuing orders for war that very year.

Ciano was warmly congratulated for the signing of the Pact, and King Victor Emmanuel of Italy emerged from his habitual reserve so far as to send him a telegram. Later, in an audience with Ciano, the King told him: "I have not sent a telegram to a minister since 1900. I thought that to break this tradition would prove to you how sincere my feelings are." The King, however, could not help adding a poisoned comment about Germany: "As long as they need us the Germans will be polite and even servile; but they will show themselves for the rabble they are at the first opportunity."

Another anecdote, which Ciano brought back from the signing of the Pact of Steel, is to be found in his diary:

"Göring had tears in his eyes when he saw the Collar of the Annunziata around Ribbentrop's neck. Mackensen told me that Göring had made a scene, saying that the Collar really belonged to him, since he was the true and only promoter of the alliance. I promised Mackensen that I would try to get Göring one."

against Greece or Tunisia. The obligation for mutual consultation between the two powers, laid down in Articles 1 and 2, must also have appeared to Ciano as sufficient guarantee—one gentleman's pledge to another.

However, Ciano did ask for three amendments to be made to the drafts:

1. The insertion into the preamble of a phrase defining the Brenner Pass as the Italo-German frontier (this clause would then clearly define the Alto Adige or South Tyrol as Italian territory);
2. The replacement of the sabre-rattling word "realisation" of living space with the word "safeguarding" [*Sicherung*];
3. The limitation of the treaty to a period of ten years.

There was no objection to these modifications, and Ciano duly set out for Berlin. When Ribbentrop met Ciano's train on May 21, he repeated to Ciano that no change had been made to the decisions reached in Milan, and he stressed that "Germany's intention is still to assure a period of peace of at least three years".

▽ *The Pact of Steel is signed and Hitler and Ciano put in a public appearance from the balcony of the New Chancellery.*

CHAPTER 5
Stalin sides with Hitler

The Pact of Steel was not 48 hours old before Hitler declared his intention of seizing the first available opportunity of settling matters with Poland once and for all. On May 23 he presided over a conference at the New Chancellery in which he addressed the Wehrmacht commanders-in-chief and chiefs-of-staff. It was at this meeting that the decision to go to war, in complete contradiction of the premises which had formed the Pact of Steel, was made.

Hitler began with a review of the current political situation and how he believed future events should be directed. The agenda had four basic points:

1. An analysis of the current political and military situation in Europe;
2. Objectives for the Wehrmacht, given this situation;
3. The probable consequences of the Wehrmacht attaining these objectives;

4. The precautions to be taken to keep all political decisions and military preparations secret, as this had to be considered an essential condition for success.

Poland was defined as Germany's Public Enemy Number One:

"The political and national unification of the German people is generally completed, with some small exceptions. Further successes can no longer be attained without bloodshed . . .

"The settling of our frontiers is a matter of military importance. The Pole is not a secondary enemy . . .

"Poland will always side with our enemies. Despite a treaty of friendship, it has always been part of Poland's intentions to turn every possible circumstance against us . . .

"Danzig is not the objective of the dispute at all. We must enlarge our living space in the East . . ."

◁ *Uneasy alliance – Hitler's pact with Stalin after so many years of anti-Communist abuse seemed too preposterous to be true, as the cartoonists were swift to point out.*
▽ *Wehrmacht commanders on manoeuvres in the spring of 1939. For them, the pact with Russia was the best news imaginable, for it meant that Germany would not have to fight a major two-front war as she had had to in 1914.*

Poland, in fact, had to be destroyed – for "living space", and to avoid the probability of her joining a hostile alliance encircling Germany. The long-term objective was the destruction of France and Great Britain, to free Germany forever from the menace of external blockade.

If the Hossbach Memorandum of November 5, 1937 was the "rough draft", Hitler's address of May 23, 1939 was the detailed blueprint for how Germany would launch World War II.

Would Russia join the Western bloc?

By the spring of 1939 the big question was the attitude of Soviet Russia. If it had come to war in 1938, the Czechs would have counted on holding out long enough for help to reach them from the French and from the Russians. When Poland became the object of German ambitions after the Prague coup in March 1939, Moscow's position became more important than ever. Here was a possible theatre of war, right on the Soviet Union's doorstep. How would Stalin react?

At first it seemed that the Soviet Union would back the cause of the Western powers. This was certainly the intention of the Soviet Foreign Commissar, Maxim Litvinov, whose policy was to contain Hitler by collective action. Three days after the Prague coup, on March 18, Litvinov proposed a six-power combination – France, Great Britain, Poland, Soviet Russia, Rumania, and Turkey – to prevent any future aggression on the part of Germany. Chamberlain, however, rejected this suggestion as "premature".

On March 23 Hitler blackmailed Lithuania into surrendering Memel and its hinterland, and Litvinov continued to press for an anti-German coalition. He cannot have been helped by Chamberlain's unilateral guarantee to Poland on March 31, which was easy to interpret as an indication that Britain would prefer an alliance with Poland to one with Soviet Russia. Litvinov made his last bid for an anti-German coalition on April 16, when he received the British Ambassador in Moscow and proposed an Anglo-Franco-Soviet mutual-assistance pact. This, too, was rejected. And on May 3 came the news that Litvinov, who had held the position since 1930, had been replaced by Vyacheslav

Molotov. It was a deeply significant move; as Germany's representative in Moscow reported to Berlin: ". . . it seems that his dismissal must be due to a spontaneous decision by Stalin . . . At the last Party Congress Stalin urged caution lest the Soviet Union be dragged into conflicts. Molotov, who is not a Jew, has the reputation of being the 'most intimate friend and closest collaborator' of Stalin. His appointment is obviously intended to provide a guarantee that foreign policy will be conducted strictly on lines laid down by Stalin."

With the Western powers vacillating again, and with this startling shift in the official outlook in Soviet foreign policy, there was every chance that Hitler could achieve a *rapprochement* with the Soviet Union. That he did so was the result not only of his own opportunism but of the co-operation of the Soviet Government itself.

The Western powers lose their chance

The replacement of Litvinov by Molotov did not cause any immediate reversal of Moscow's attitude. Stalin still wanted to reach agreement with Britain and France – but only on equal terms. It soon became apparent that the prospects of such a coalition were jeopardised by Poland's unwillingness to conclude a mutual defence pact with Soviet Russia. Added to this was Chamberlain's obvious preference for a direct alliance with Poland. In fact, Stalin's position was simple. He had to safeguard Soviet Russia from the consequences of a probable German attack on Poland, but he was not prepared to enter into any agreement with the Western powers without receiving full co-operation from them.

Molotov asked for a representative of the British Government to go to Moscow for talks. But whereas Chamberlain had had no hesitation in flying to Germany in person for meetings with Hitler, he considered it sufficient now to send William Strang, an able official but one virtually unknown outside the British Foreign Office. Strang arrived in Moscow in the middle of June. Not surprisingly, Stalin and Molotov were put out at having to deal with a minor official; not surprisingly either, the talks got nowhere, and on July 23 Molotov proposed that Britain and

△ *Soviet Foreign Commissar Maxim Litvinov, whose policy was to contain Germany by collective action with the Western powers. The cautious vacillation of Britain and France ruined his hopes and led to his dismissal in early May 1939.*
▷ *Stalin with his close confidant, Vyacheslav Molotov, who replaced Litvinov. Molotov, too, found that Soviet Russia had little to expect in the way of concrete proposals from the West.*

„Meine Herren, die Sowjets bieten Ihnen nochmals Hilfe an!" — „Thank you, Mister Litwinow, wenn Sie wegbleiben, ist schon viel geholfen!"

△ *German cartoon (from the magazine* Simplicissimus*) sneers at the Franco-British attitude towards Soviet Russia. Litvinov's proposals are rejected with the comment that Russia will be more help if she stays out. It was only too true: the Franco-British lack of interest in a defensive alliance with Moscow led directly to the Soviet-German Non-Aggression Pact.*

France send a military mission to Russia.

This duly arrived, but in an extremely leisurely fashion. The mission—with Admiral Sir Reginald Drax representing Britain and General Joseph Doumenc France—travelled by ship to Leningrad and only arrived in Moscow on August 11. Here, again, was an apparent affront. Before their arrival neither representative had been heard of in Moscow. More than this, Drax had not only been given no powers to negotiate, but also told to "go very slowly with the military negotiations, watching the progress of the political negotiations". The Soviet verdict, in the official *History of the Great Patriotic War*,

was severe: "When B. M. Shaposhnikov [Red Army Chief of the General Staff] said that the Soviet Union was ready to make available against the aggressor 120 infantry divisions, 16 cavalry divisions, 5,000 medium and heavy guns, 9,000 to 10,000 tanks, and 5,000 to 5,500 bomber and fighter planes, General Heywood, a member of the British Mission, talked about one mechanised and five infantry divisions. This in itself was enough to suggest a frivolous British attitude to the talks with the Soviet Union."

The Soviet leaders did not hide their displeasure at this apparently casual approach, and Drax was obliged to contact London and request full credentials. But by the time these arrived, on August 21, the Germans had seized their chance.

It seemed unbelievable to Hitler and Ribbentrop that the Western powers would fritter away their chances of bringing the Soviet Union into their camp, but they were swift to seize their opportunity and did not make the same mistakes as Chamberlain and Daladier. Even before the dismissal of Litvinov, there had been discussions on the prospects of improving German-Soviet relations, and these continued throughout May, June, and July with the balance swinging more and more in favour of the Germans. Ribbentrop stressed that there were "no differences" between Berlin and Moscow which could not be solved easily. He expressed his desire to reach first an economic and later a political agreement with the Soviet Union, and stated that he was willing to go to Moscow in person for discussions. Here was an attitude very different from that displayed by Britain and France—and Stalin welcomed it eagerly.

By the middle of August the military discussions in Moscow had reached a crux: would Poland permit troops to operate on her territory in the event of war with Germany in which Soviet Russia would side with Poland, Britain, and France? Here everthing turned on Beck's deeply-rooted anti-Russian bias. Bonnet urged him to give way on this point, but Beck refused. And on August 20, the day of the Polish refusal, Marshal Edward Rydz-Smigly, the Polish Commander-in-Chief, made the fatal statement which confirmed every Russian suspicion that the Western powers were insincere: "With the Germans we would risk losing our liberty. With the Russians we would lose our soul." It was now too late for France and Britain to conclude an agreement with Russia, but such was Daladier's desire for one that on the next day he sent a telegram to the members of the French mission in Moscow authorising them to sign a military agreement, presumably as the British Ambassador in Warsaw had managed to obtain a preliminary agreement from the Polish Government. There is no proof for this, but in any case Voroshilov replied that the French had no right to conclude an agreement for another sovereign nation. In fact, Polish concurrence with the agreement was not sought until later.

Soviet Russia had, in fact, taken the easy way out without waiting for Poland's refusal. Churchill's memoirs contain an interesting account of Russia's attitude in 1939, given in Stalin's own words. When Churchill visited Moscow in August 1942, Stalin had explained to him how things had been in 1939. " 'We formed the opinion,' said Stalin, 'that the British and French Governments were not resolved to go to war if Poland were attacked, but that they hoped the diplomatic line-up of Great Britain, France, and Russia would deter Hitler. We were sure it would not.'

" 'How many divisions,' Stalin had asked, 'will France send against Germany on mobilisation?' The answer was, 'About a hundred.' He then asked, 'How many will England send?' The answer was, 'Two, and two later.' 'Ah, two, and two later,' Stalin had repeated. 'Do you know,' he asked, 'how many divisions we shall have to put on the Russian front if we go to war with Germany?' There was a pause. 'More than three hundred.' "

Did Hitler bully Stalin into acquiescence?

Those who support Stalin's decisions in 1939 have argued that Hitler bullied Stalin into signing the Nazi-Soviet Non-Aggression Pact of August 1939 with a tacit ultimatum, implying that Soviet Russia would be considered an enemy of Germany if events should result in a military showdown with Poland. But there is no evidence of this in Hitler's telegram to Stalin on August 20. Its message is clear: Hitler did

△ Marshal Rydz-Smigly, the Polish C.-in-C. His downright refusal to allow Soviet troops to enter Poland in the event of a German invasion gave the kiss of death to the military negotiations in Moscow.
◁ The Franco-British military mission sets out. Its leisurely journey to Russia by sea, and the comparative obscurity of its leaders – Doumenc for France and Drax for Britain – caused yet more disenchantment in the Kremlin and the talks took a long time to get nowhere.

△ *German "top brass" watch a parade in Berlin*. Left to right: *Himmler, Reichsführer-S.S.; Keitel, chief of staff of the O.K.W. or Armed forces High Command; Brauchitsch, C.-in-C of the German Army; Raeder, C.-in-C. of the* Kriegsmarine, *the German Navy.*
▷ *"Fascism means war!" screams this Russian anti-German poster of 1936. The complete reversal of the traditional hostility between Germany and Russia with the signing of the 1939 Pact astonished the world.*

not state that the Soviet Union would be involved in Germany's quarrel with Poland –he did not blackmail Stalin at all. In Paragraph 5 of the telegram, Hitler announced that Germany's march on Poland could be provoked at any time: "The tension between Poland and Germany has become intolerable, and Poland's current attitude means that a crisis may arise any day. Faced with such arrogance, Germany has already decided to safeguard the interests of the Reich with every resource at her disposal."

Hitler's telegram concluded: "In my opinion, it is desirable, in view of the intention of the two states to enter into a new relationship, not to lose any time. For this reason I would like you to talk to my Foreign Minister again on Tuesday, August 22, or at the latest on the 23rd. The Reich Foreign Minister will have full and extraordinary powers to reach agreement on a non-aggression pact."

Where is the threat? There is none. Not even Hitler's conversation with Generals Halder and von Brauchitsch on August 14, faithfully recorded by Halder, reveals any hint of putting pressure on Stalin.

Stalin's conditions

Paradoxical as it may seem, then, Stalin and Molotov did not yield to any pressure from Hitler and Ribbentrop. On the contrary, it was the latter who followed the line laid down by Moscow. As early as May 20, Molotov had told Count Friedrich von der Schulenburg, the German Ambassador in Moscow, that it would be impossible for the Soviet Union to embark on economic negotiations with Germany until some measure of "political understanding" had been reached.

Here, in fact, was the origin of the Non-Aggression Pact of August 23. Stalin did not grant Hitler the benefit of Russia's benevolent neutrality without imposing a final condition. On August 19, Molotov had read to Schulenburg a draft, five-article pact, containing the provision that "the present pact shall be valid only if a special protocol is signed simultaneously covering the points in which the High Contracting Parties are interested in the field of foreign policy. This protocol must

be an integral part of the pact."

Hitler granted this request without even
discussing it, and no more obstacles remained. Stalin's telegram inviting Ribbentrop to Moscow to sign the pact arrived on
the 21st. Albert Speer remembers: "During dinner a note was handed to Hitler.
He read it through quickly, stared for a
moment, turned red with emotion, and
then banged on the table, making the
glasses rattle. In a high-pitched voice he
exclaimed: 'I've got them! I've got them!'"
Ribbentrop flew to Moscow on the 23rd
and signed both the Pact and Protocol in
an atmosphere of great cordiality. The
Pact itself was a conventional statement
of non-aggression, but the text of the
Protocol, which was revealed only in 1948,
shows it for what it was: one of the shab-
biest and most immoral agreements of all
time.

Soviet leaders have stated that the Pact
was not in conflict with other treaties
already signed by the Soviet Union, but
in fact the Russo-Polish Non-Aggression
Pact of 1932 stipulated that in the event

of one of the parties being attacked by a
third party, the other was to remain
neutral.

The conditions of the secret Protocol
speak for themselves:

"On the occasion of the signature of the
Non-Aggression Pact between the German
Reich and the Union of Soviet Socialist
Republics the undersigned plenipotentiaries of each of the two parties discussed
in strictly confidential conversations the
question of the boundary of their respective spheres of influence in Eastern Europe.
These conversations led to the following
conclusions:

1. In the event of a territorial and politica[l]
    rearrangement in the areas belonging
    to the Baltic States (Finland, Estonia,
    Latvia, and Lithuania) the norther[n]
    boundary of Lithuania shall represen[t]
    the boundary between the spheres o[f]
    interest of Germany and the U.S.S.R.

2. In the event of territorial and politica[l]
    rearrangement of the areas belonging
    to the Polish State, the spheres of in-
    fluence of Germany and the U.S.S.R[.]

shall be bounded approximately by the line of the Narew, Vistula, and San rivers.

The question of whether the interests of both parties make desirable the maintenance of an independent Polish state and how such a state should be bounded can only be definitely determined in the course of further political developments. In any event both Governments will resolve this question by means of friendly agreement.

3. With regard to South-Eastern Europe attention is called by the Soviet side to its interest in Bessarabia. The German side declares its complete political disinterestedness in these areas.

4. This Protocol shall be treated by both Parties as strictly secret."

▽ *Gifted amateur and hardbitten professional: Hitler and Gerd von Rundstedt discuss troop concentrations. Rundstedt would lead the southern German army group when the time came to settle accounts with Poland.*

No time to haggle

Since August 16, there had been an extraordinary contrast between the haste shown by the Germans and the temporising attitude of the Russians. This, combined with the date of the agreement, August 23, supports the argument that Stalin and Molotov were setting the pace in the negotiations. Ribbentrop was in Moscow for only 25 hours, and he signed the Pact within hours of touching down at the airport. In those 25 hours he had also had to squeeze in two hasty meals at the German Embassy and his journeys to and from the Kremlin–not to mention the impromptu celebrations and toast-drinkings after the ceremony and a brief sleep on the night of August 23–24 before his departure at 1325 hours on the 24th. Thus there was little time to discuss last-minute amendments to the draft pact (such as Stalin's inquiry as to whether or not the ports of Windau and Libau would fall within the Russian sphere of influence). Ribbentrop must therefore have signed the Pact as it stood. There was, of course, a perfectly good reason why Ribbentrop's hands were tied: Hitler had brought forward the date for the invasion of Poland and fixed it for dawn on the 26th, thus giving Ribbentrop no time to waste.

When Stalin and Molotov agreed to meet Ribbentrop on the 23rd, did they in fact know how compliant he would be because of the time factor? More important, was Hitler trapped into acting more in the interests of the Soviet Union than of Germany?

Russia's decision: "concrete action" against Poland

On September 4–the fourth day after Germany had taken the plunge and attacked Poland–Schulenburg, on Ribbentrop's instructions, asked Molotov:

"1. Would the U.S.S.R. object if, to hasten the destruction of the Polish Army, the Wehrmacht were to conduct operations in the Soviet sphere of influence?

2. Would the U.S.S.R. not consider it desirable to send Russian forces in good time into the zone of influence defined for the U.S.S.R. in Polish territory?"

The following day Molotov sent Ribbentrop his telegrammed reply, via Schulenburg. "We agree with you on the absolute necessity for us to take concrete action. We feel, however, that the moment for this has not yet come. We may be proved wrong, but we feel that excessive haste may prejudice our interests by helping to unite our adversaries. We believe that as operations develop one or both of our two powers may well be momentarily obliged to cross the demarcation line between our respective spheres of influence. But considerations of this nature must not prevent the strict execution of the envisaged plan."

This document suggests that during the discussions on August 23 a plan was adopted by mutual agreement which implied the Soviet Union taking "concrete action" against Poland. All this was in complete contrast with Molotov's statements on the evening of August 22, when he had told the French Ambassador "that the fundamental policy of the U.S.S.R. remains unchanged: to keep the peace and resist aggression. The Soviet Government, as France's representative in Moscow can attest, has already signed several non-aggression pacts, including one with Poland. In agreeing to negotiate with Germany, the U.S.S.R. has no intention of departing from this essentially peaceful attitude."

Such was Soviet Russia's claim, and since then Soviet historians have argued that in dealing with Hitler, Stalin was trying to buy time to reorganise and re-equip his armies. But this argument overlooks the 136 infantry and cavalry divisions, the 5,000 medium and heavy guns, the 9,000 to 10,000 tanks, and the 5,000 to 5,500 aircraft which Voroshilov and Shaposhnikov had described to General Doumenc and Admiral Drax (unless the figures were grossly inflated). In any case, if Russia were so weak, her leaders had brought her to the brink of destruction and defeat with their lack of foresight. On September 1, 1939, a coalition of the Soviet Union, Poland, France, and Britain could have unleashed 270 divisions against Germany's 108.

On June 22, 1941, the German Army totalled 208 divisions, of which 55 were tied down in secondary theatres. But by then the Wehrmacht had received the aid of 50 satellite divisions and brigades, and could therefore throw 203 divisions against the Russian 176.

△ *After the signing of the German-Soviet Pact in Moscow on August 23, 1939, Stalin proposes Hitler's health and clinks glasses with Heinrich Hoffmann, the Führer's personal photographer.*

„Nimmer wird das Reich zerstöret — wenn ihr einig seid und treu"

1 Nationalsozialisten

The Making of a Dictator
Adolf Hitler

On September 12, 1919, Adolf Hitler, an Austrian-born corporal in a Bavarian regiment in the German Army, attended a meeting of the German Workers' Party in Munich. Hitler had gone to the meeting as a spy for the army; he left it convinced that in this party he had found the vehicle that could raise him to supreme power.

Germany after World War I was a political void – small parties flourished and then faded under a government that could only survive with the army's support. Hitler felt that he could exploit this, and joined the German Workers' Party as its fifth member on September 14. He worked for the party in his off duty moments while he was still in the army, but in April 1920 he left the army and went to work for the party as a full time propagandist, building up its membership and

gradually usurping the leadership. Soon after it became the German National Socialist Workers' Party (*Nationalsozialistische Deutsche Arbeiterpartei*, N.S.D. A.P.) or Nazi Party in August 1920, Hitler was made its undisputed leader.

The message of the Nazi Party was simple and direct: it would restore Germany's prosperity and position as a world power and would utterly crush the Jewish- and Communist-backed world conspiracy which had led to the "undefeated" German Army being "stabbed in the back" by German socialism in 1918. The message was simple: the means of putting it across was brutal, direct, and efficient. Hitler had a natural genius for mob oratory, and had realised that the way to get results was to pitch the message on an emotional rather than an intellectual level, and

gear it to the most stupid elements of the audience. The message was driven home by endless repetition, the violence of the speeches, and the violence carried into the meetings and into the streets by the Nazi "brown-shirt" militia, the *Sturmabteilungen* or S.A., commanded by an ex-army staff officer, Ernst Röhm. The task of these thugs was to crush as ruthlessly as possible any heckling in Nazi meetings and to beat up the opposition in the streets.

The party continued to grow, and in November 1923 Hitler felt that the time was ripe for the Nazis to seize power in Munich. In this venture he had the support of General Erich Ludendorff, second in command of the German Army at the end of the war, support which Hitler hoped would persuade the army not to intervene. He could not have been more wrong. The armed up-

Führer wir folgen Dir! Alle sagen Ja!

control. The new approach's success can be gauged from the growing membership of the Nazi Party: in 1925 25,000 and in 1928 110,000. In the elections of 1928 the Nazis polled 800,000 out of 31 million votes, enough to secure 12 out of 491 seats in the Reichstag, the German parliament.

Then once again world economics played into Hitler's hands. In 1929 the Wall Street Crash and the subsequent world Depression handed Hitler the German working class. The results were startling: in the first year of the Depression the membership of the party almost doubled, and though the Communist Party also benefited, the Nazis were better placed to exploit their success.

The Weimar Republic was entirely unable to cope with the crisis, and after the defeat of a minority government in the summer of 1930, new elections were scheduled for September. The Nazis polled 6½ million votes and won 107 seats. They were unable to use their new-found power, however, as the Chancellor, Brüning, ruled by decree. By the end of 1931, party membership had passed the 5 million mark.

Hitler's next move was to contest the Presidency in the spring of 1932. Hitler came second to the aged German World War I hero, Hindenburg, but secured 37 per cent of the vote. The next few months witnessed a bewildering succession of events. Franz von Papen, not even a member of the Reichstag, became Chancellor, and in the elections which followed, the Nazis polled 14 million votes and won 230 seats, to make them the largest party in the Reichstag. But Hindenburg, on the advice of General von Schleicher, the army's political chief, only offered Hitler the Vice-Chancellorship, which he refused. After another election and two offers of the Chancellorship in coalition governments, the intrigues of Schleicher finally persuaded Hindenburg to make Hitler Chancellor on January 30, 1933. The last stage in Hitler's rise to power had begun.

The new government was only, however, an interim one pending new elections, but once again fate played into Hitler's hands. On February 27 the Reichstag was burned down. It seems likely that a Dutch Communist was responsible, but Hitler quickly laid the blame at the German Communists' door. In the subsequent anti-Communist panic which

rising, subsequently named the "Beer-Hall" *Putsch* after the beer-garden from which Hitler and Ludendorff started at the head of their 3,000 followers on November 9, was a complete disaster. The army was ordered in to halt the insurrection, and in the fighting, 16 Nazis were killed. Hitler and Ludendorff were arrested and tried for treason. Ludendorff was freed. Hitler received a five-year gaol sentence.

Paradoxically enough, it was the trial that was the making of the Nazis. Hitler dominated the trial with his personality and speaking, and emerged as an international figure, receiving also, more importantly, the bonus of a great deal of free publicity in Germany.

Eventually, Hitler served only nine months of his sentence, just enough time to write his political testament, *Mein Kampf* ("My Struggle"), with the aid of his deputy, Rudolf Hess.

The failure of the *Putsch* had made Hitler realise that, despite his rabid hatred of democracy, he would have to use it to come to the position of power from which he could then destroy it. This revelation coincided with a change in Nazi policy necessitated by the altering economic situation. Previously, Nazi propaganda had been geared to the working class, which had been worst hit by the depression after the war. But the upswing in the Weimar Republic's economy in the middle 1920's created full employment again. So Hitler switched his campaign to the middle classes, whose savings had been wiped out in the post-war inflation and who did not profit from the new boom. Thus Hitler set about building up the party on a solid basis of the middle class, industrialists, and financiers, to whom he offered the carrot of greater profits once the Communists had been disposed of and the working class brought under

◁ ◁ *"Führer, we follow you! All say Yes!" A Nazi propaganda poster urges the German people to vote "yes" in the plebiscite held on August 19, 1934. This was to find whether or not they wished to see the functions of the President and of the Chancellor made one in the person of the Führer, Adolf Hitler, the leader of Germany. Hitler's policy was completely justified by a massive vote of 88.2 per cent in his favour.*

▽ *Party standard bearers at the Nuremberg "Party Day" Rally in 1933. Amid all this para-military splendour and discipline, Hitler had the chance to practise his genius for mass oratory before a spell-bound audience.*

▷ *A knight in shining armour? The subtitle of this poster – "riding towards the East" – gives an indication that even at this date, 1936, it should have been possible to see that Hitler's ultimate goal lay not in western Europe but in the East, in Poland and in Russia.*

swept the country, the Nazis triumphed in the elections of March 5 with 17 million votes, 44 per cent of those cast.

On March 21 the new Reichstag met in the garrison church at Potsdam. It was the beginning of its last session, for the Nazi majority voted through an Enabling Act on the 23rd. This gave Hitler the right to legislate on matters of finance, foreign affairs, and the constitution. Hitler was now firmly established as Germany's leader. All he had to do was to gather in the last elements of power not already in his hands.

All political parties (except the Nazis), the trade unions, and all employers' associations were abolished. And the old federal constitution of the nation was replaced by a system of Nazi provinces or *gaus*.

Next, Hitler purged his party. He had long been worried by the ambitions of Röhm and the dissidence of the Strasser brothers, Gregor and Otto, who had been in the party from the beginning, but were now worried about the

swing away from true socialism. On June 30, 1934, Hitler did away with all his opponents in the "Night of the Long Knives". Hitler's personal bodyguard, the *Schutzstaffeln* or S.S., led by Heinrich Himmler, murdered Röhm, the Strassers, Schleicher, and many others whom Hitler and his chief minister, Hermann Göring, had decided to eliminate. Hitler's total supremacy within the party was now completely assured.

The last obstacle to Hitler's absolute power was removed on August 2, 1934, when Hindenburg died. The office of President was abolished and its functions amalgamated with those of the Chancellor in the new position of *Führer*. The army then swore allegiance to Hitler personally, and finally a plebiscite on the 19th gave Hitler an overwhelming vote of approval. The task of purging Germany could now begin in earnest, and then Germany would be ready to turn her attention to fulfilling Hitler's vast territorial ambitions.

◁ ◁ *Hitler reviews the standards of his private armies, the S.A. and S.S. Beyond Hitler, in a cap, can be seen the S.S. leader Heinrich Himmler.*
▽ *"We won't stand for any sabotage of the Führer's work." As clear as the message is the threat of punishment – by the squad of S.A. in the lorry.*
▷ *A Reich Labour Service poster – "We are creating Life and Spirit".*
▷ ▽ *Ten years of the National Socialist German Students' League commemorated. It was organisations of this kind that provided the S.A. with its pseudo-intellectual thugs.*
▷ ▽ ▽ *Propaganda for a plebiscite decision to unite Germany and Austria as "Greater Germany".*
▷ ▷ *Hermann Göring, figurehead of Germany's economic miracle and head of her air force.*
▷ ▷ ▽ *Joseph Goebbels, the masterful Reich Propaganda Minister, and after Hitler, perhaps the most intelligent and influential figure in the Nazi Party.*

Count-down to war

△ *June 1939, and thousands of Germans are treated to an epic night-time parade proclaiming the armed strength of the Reich.*

On August 22, when Stalin had agreed to Ribbentrop's visit to Moscow, Hitler called a meeting, at the Berghof, of the Wehrmacht's senior commanders, to brief them on the current situation, give them their orders, and try to instill in them some of his "savage resolution". Even in these solemn, if not tragic, circumstances there was a comic element: Göring. His appearance on this occasion made a vivid impression on General Erich von Manstein, who recalled it in detail afterwards. "Over a white, open-necked shirt he wore a green, sleeveless leather jerkin with big yellow leather buttons. He wore grey shorts, and long grey stockings strained over his massive calves. Enormous shoes added to the frivolous appearance of his costume. But most splendid of all was a big red and gold belt draped round his belly, from which hung a hunting-knife in a scabbard of red leather ornamented with gold."

At this meeting, notes were taken by Admiral Hermann Böhm, Fleet-Commander, which preserved the essential points made by Hitler in his harangue. Hitler started by describing the key personalities whose attitudes favoured Germany and made it inadvisable for Germany to delay any longer in settling accounts with Poland. First came Hitler himself. "He had united the German people. He possessed a measure of confidence and a weight of authority which any successor would find difficult to match. But at any moment he could be disposed of by an enemy bullet, mental failure, or disease. As far as the solution of the problems of the German people was concerned, his life was a factor of the highest importance."

After Hitler himself, Mussolini. "With Italy treaties did not matter, but personalities. Mussolini assured the maintenance of the alliance; although one had doubts about what he might do, his achievements spoke for themselves. Mussolini was a man without nerves. If proof was wanted, one had only to think of Abyssinia."

Franco, too, was an important man. Admittedly, all Hitler wanted from Spain was a benevolent neutrality, but Hitler judged that Franco alone was strong enough to resist partisan influences from within Spain.

As far as the Reich's enemies were concerned, it was Germany's good fortune that the men holding their reins of power were mediocre vacillators rather than leaders of a stature comparable with Hitler's own. Moreover, France and Britain would find themselves seriously hampered by other factors in bringing any effective help to Poland during the attack that was about to break upon her.

In the Far East, Great Britain was neutralised by Japan. In the Mediterranean, after the conquest of Albania, she was held in check by Italy, as was France. The R.A.F.'s manpower was only a third of the Luftwaffe's. As for the British land forces, the five or six divisions (if that) which Britain could put into the field were a drop in the ocean. From all these points Hitler found himself bound to conclude: "It seems to me impossible that any responsible British statesman dare, under these conditions, accept the risks of open warfare."

Nor was France any better off. The deficiencies of her armaments and the lack of sufficient recruits of military age meant that she would be unable to endure the cost of a long-term war. It was unlikely that France would hurl her army, accustomed as it was to the strategy of defending the Maginot Line, against the strong-points of the Siegfried Line; without any guarantee of success, the French High Command would have to risk 250,000 men in an operation of this nature. Neither Paris nor London, argued Hitler, would dream of invading Germany via neutral territory. "Switzerland would fire at any power who violated her neutrality. Holland would observe a strict neutrality for fear that Japan, should she become involved, would threaten the Dutch colonies in the Far East. Belgium would also remain strictly neutral: in World War I she had the searing experience of acting as the principal battle-ground without gaining any profit whatsoever." All these considerations made up Hitler's thesis that "the probability of the Western powers intervening in the conflict is a small one".

Hitler's one fear: another Munich

It was true, Hitler continued, that Great Britain and France could counter the invasion of Poland by recalling their ambassadors from Berlin and blockading Germany. But this possibility, which he had already discussed with Generals von Brauchitsch and Halder on August 14, would be countered by the non-aggression pact which was to be signed the following day in Moscow. Germany, in fact, could now prepare for the conflict without having to plan for a two-front war. According to a document produced in evidence at Nuremberg after the war, the authenticity of which has been questioned, Hitler exclaimed: "I have struck from the hands of the West the weapon which Soviet help would have given them. The possibility now exists of inflicting a mortal blow on Poland. Everything now shows that the path is open for the soldier," adding: "My only fear is that some *schweinehund* will make a proposal for mediation!"

Hermann Göring, ex World-War I ace, was a ruthless but able tough who rose to the status of "Number Two" in the Nazi hierarchy – Hitler's successor. He took a prominent part in the "Night of the Long Knives" in June 1934. With the admission of German re-armament in 1935, Goring was made Minister for Air and C.-in-C. of the Luftwaffe. He was also in charge of the Nazi 4-Year Plan from 1936. He was promoted to Field-Marshal in 1938 and to Reichsmarschall in 1940.

It is clear that Hitler's words were very favourably received by the generals and admirals present. The conclusion of the non-aggression pact seemed a masterstroke, saving Germany from the danger of a war on two fronts which had confronted Kaiser Wilhelm II some 25 years before. None of them doubted that Poland could be defeated in 15 days or three weeks, provided that France and Great Britain did not intervene. In which case, surely the Western democracies would once again resign themselves to a *fait accompli*?

△ Le Rire *cartoon on the nemesis of German rearmament: a Nazi family cowers in its air-raid shelter while the mother glowers at Hitler's picture. "You can tell he's got no sons."*
▽ Simplicissimus *ridicules John Bull and the Polish Eagle: "Should I let him fly or shouldn't I?"*
▷ *Ciano and Ribbentrop, Foreign Ministers of the Italo-German partnership, cutting considerably less of a dash in civilian clothes than in their flamboyant, para-military uniforms.*

How could France help Poland?

Hitler's arguments had a lot to be said for them, but in fact he was making the fatal mistake of thinking that his enemies would see things in the same light. From this mistake would come the war, first European and later world-wide, which

Hitler believed had been made impossible by the German-Soviet Non-Aggression Pact.

In Paris, the news of the imminent conclusion of the pact, which had come as a great surprise, caused Bonnet, with Daladier's consent, to call a meeting of the Committee of National Defence on August 23. Those present included the Ministers, the Chief-of-Staff for National Defence (General Maurice Gamelin), the C.-in-C., French Navy (Admiral Jean Darlan), the C.-in-C., *Armée de l'Air* or French Air Force (General Joseph Vuillemin), the Army and Air Force Chiefs-of-Staff (Colson and Têtu), and the Secretary-General to the War Office (Jacomet).

Given the new circumstance of the Moscow Pact, for which Poland was partially responsible, it had to be decided whether or not France should revise her relations with her allies in Eastern and South-Eastern Europe. In Daladier's opinion, the need for this decision led to the following questions:

"1. Could France, without intervening, passively accept the removal from the map of Europe of Poland and Rumania, or of one of these powers?

2. What means were at France's disposal to prevent this?

3. What measures should be taken?"

The first question being essentially a military one, it fell to Gamelin to reply, and his view was simple. "Asked what sort of resistance Poland and Rumania would be able to put up, he said that he expected Poland to make an honourable resistance which would tie down the main armies of Germany, preventing them from turning against us until spring, by which time England would be at our side."

When questioned as to Rumania's powers of resistance, Gamelin was not able to be so precise. This would depend on the attitudes which Yugoslavia and Hungary adopted in the event of war. Gamelin insisted, however, on the importance of Italy's continued neutrality, in which he was energetically supported by Admiral Darlan.

Would it be necessary, in fact, for France to agree to another compromise in order to gain the time which might be needed to confront Germany on better terms? The Committee of National Defence said no, and elaborated its reason: "After much discussion, it is clear that if we will be stronger in a few months, Germany will be as well, especially as she will have all the resources of Poland and Rumania at her disposal."

In consequence, France had no choice. "The only solution to be considered is that of keeping our agreements with regard to Poland, despite the fact that they were made before the negotiations with the U.S.S.R." As for France's military readiness, Air Minister Guy La Chambre showed himself wildly optimistic, both about France's large-scale production of modern fighters and about the R.A.F.'s capacity to carry out "massive bombing raids" on North Germany. He was also confident in the French Air Force's ability to co-operate with the ground forces. The Navy was ready, Admiral Darlan declared; this was perfectly true. And so, said Gamelin, was the Army.

Gamelin has often been blamed for making erroneous claims about the French Army's efficiency at the outbreak of war in 1939. This accusation, he stated later, is a misleading interpretation of what he actually said on August 23: he was only stating that the mechanism for mobilisation and troop concentration was ready. And he added: "A modern army is never ready. Neither the French Army nor the German Army was ready in 1914... In 1939 Germany was ready to attack Poland: she was not ready to attack France. In 1940 she was not ready to attack England. On the eve of battle you rarely have all the *matériel* you asked for." What is more,

Gamelin emphasised constantly during the meeting that France could put only 120 divisions into the field against Germany's 200.

Should Gamelin carry the blame for having misled the French Government as to the fighting efficiency of the French Army? This is the view taken by Georges Bonnet in his memoirs, but it goes too far. All the documents made available in 1945 show that the Committee of National Defence was not mistaken in its conclusions on August 23, 1939, and that Hitler's chances would have been much greater in 1943 or 1944 than in 1939.

What would Britain's reaction have been if the French Government and its military advisers had reached a different decision? Relations between Paris and London remained excellent–but there can be no doubt that they would not have survived a French suggestion for another Munich. Soviet Russia's ill-judged adherence to the Reich made absolutely no difference to the resolution of the British Government, Parliament, and public.

On August 25 Lord Halifax, British Foreign Secretary, and Count Edward Raczyński, Ambassador Extraordinary and Plenipotentiary of the Polish Republic in London, signed a Mutal Assistance Pact. Article 1 of this agreement defined the basis of agreement between the two powers: "If one of the contracting Parties

△ *Military discussions between France and Poland took place in May 1939. Here General Gamelin* (centre), *French supreme commander, confers with General Kasprzycki* (right), *Polish War Minister. The Poles did not take the advice of the French not to attempt to defend the Danzig Corridor and the regions west of the Vistula– with fatal results.*

△ △ *During Italian Army manoeuvres at San Marinella, Hitler and Mussolini separate for individual discussions.* △ *Foreign observers at the San Marinella manoeuvres, which were intended to impress the Western powers with the armed might of Italy.*

finds itself engaged in hostilities with a European power as a result of aggression by that power, the other contracting Party will give immediate help to the Party engaged in hostilities with every source in its power." The possibility of this treaty, which had been decided upon as early as

April 1939, had been one of the major stumbling blocks in the negotiations between the Western powers and the Soviet Union during the summer of 1939.

Article 2 covered the eventuality of indirect aggression: Britain undertook to take up arms if Poland were obliged to use force to counter any action which represented an indirect threat to her independence (such as Danzig). But Poland undertook the same obligation if Britain should have to go to war to safeguard the independence or neutrality of another European state, which meant, although they were not named, the Netherlands, Belgium, and Switzerland.

To last for five years, the Anglo-Polish Treaty of Mutual Assistance, according to its concluding Article 8, came into force from the moment of its signature. A secret protocol, not revealed until much later, specified Germany as the major enemy.

In Berlin, the news that Britain and Poland had concluded such an agreement was a stunning blow, although Chamberlain, as early as August 22, had written to Hitler informing him in no uncertain terms that Britain would honour her earlier assurance to Poland. Every argument which Hitler had put to his generals and admirals at the Berghof on the 22nd had been proved wrong. Informed of the treaty on the afternoon of the 25th, Hitler decided to give himself time to think, and at 1930 hours he gave instructions that O.K.W. be telephoned and ordered to call off the attack on Poland and pull back its troops to the German frontier.

"Y"-Day, as the Germans called it, had been fixed for the morning of August 26, and H-Hour for 0030. At 2030 hours on the 25th, the German army group commanders had been told of the counter-order and had immediately passed it on to their subordinates. But all this took time to reach the front line troops. It was possible to halt most of the troops in the centre, but not on the flanks, where certain patrols were already in action on Polish territory. This led to violent incidents on the frontier of East Prussia and also on the Jablonika Pass, an important point in the Carpathians on the Polish-Slovak frontier, where the *Brandenburg* special operations unit, which had been trained to create "incidents", was operating.

Cold feet in Italy

While Great Britain had thrown in her lot with Poland, Ciano was trying to prevent Italy from being dragged into war by the terms of the Pact of Steel. The German-Soviet Non-Aggression Pact had come as a total surprise to the Italians, and the intervention of the Western powers seemed

△ *German troops, ready for action in Poland. August 26 was Hitler's original "D-Day" for Poland: the invasion was called off at the eleventh hour, but not before some German units had clashed with the Polish frontier forces.*
◁ *Berlin's* Lustige Blätter *shows Churchill—ace warmonger in German eyes—playing Grave Digger to Chamberlain's Hamlet on the brink of a new world holocaust. "To be or not to be . . ."*

certain to Ciano. This would therefore mean a general war, which Hitler and Ribbentrop had assured him in May would not come about until 1943 or 1944 at the earliest. Considering the sorry state of the Italian Army and Air Force, Ciano believed that it would be folly for Italy to go to war

△ *New York's* Saturday Evening Post *caricatures the growing talk of war and Mussolini's "non-belligerence" policy.*
▽ *Bernardo Attolico (right), Mussolini's Ambassador in Berlin, who brought Hitler the Duce's message that Italy would be unable to go to war in support of Germany, unless she received massive supplies of weapons and raw materials from the Reich. It was this bombshell that prompted Hitler to postpone his war until Italy's position had been clarified.*

with France and Great Britain, especially as Germany would be concentrating the majority of her forces against Poland.

Mussolini, on whom so much depended, found it impossible to consider affairs with any detachment or assurance. Ciano's daily record in his Diary shows Mussolini at his worst: hesitant, open to any form of influence, constantly deceived by his generals, bitter against everyone, yielding to his contradictory impulses in misinformed outbursts, and generally trying to play a rôle inconsistent with his poor health. He could find no fault in Ciano's argument that Hitler and Ribbentrop had made a mockery of the Pact of Steel; he knew all the faults in the Italian war machine; and he also knew that it would be impossible to put them right quickly without the raw materials needed. But he believed that while neutrality might be fitting for small nations like Belgium or Switzerland it was unworthy for a great imperial power like Fascist Italy. He also felt that to remain neutral would damage his reputation both at home and abroad.

Mussolini backs down

On August 25, however, Ciano and Mussolini reached a compromise, and Mussolini informed Hitler in the evening that "it would be better if I did not take the *initiative* in military operations in view of the *present* situation of Italian war preparations. Our intervention can, however, take place at once if Germany delivers to us immediately the military supplies and raw materials to resist the attack which the French and English would direct against us."

At the moment that French Ambassador Coulondre left Hitler's presence after handing over the solemn warning of the French Government, Italy's Ambassador, Bernardo Attolico, arrived with Mussolini's message that Italy was not ready for war. (It had been Attolico who had told Coulondre on the 25th that Hitler had made the decision for war, and thus enabled the latter to inform his minister of the fact immediately.) Interpreter Schmidt later recalled that "this letter was a bombshell. Hitler was wounded and deeply shaken by the sudden *volte-face*, which he had not expected. With an icy expression he dismissed Mussolini's representative, telling him that there would be a reply very soon. 'The Italians are behaving just as they did in 1914,' he de-

clared once the door had closed. And the corridors of the Chancellery echoed with unfavourable comments on the disloyal Axis partner.

"General Keitel came in hastily. And a few moments later we heard that the go-ahead for the attack on Poland had been countermanded."

On Berlin's request, the Italians devoted August 26 to drawing up a list of their country's needs. Ciano urged the military chiefs to omit nothing, and they did not fail him. "It's enough to kill a bull, if a bull could read," he noted happily. Nor was he exaggerating.

Italy requested 150 batteries of anti-aircraft guns and an unspecified number of other weapons. The raw materials which Germany was asked to send to Italy–to serve the needs of one year of war–totalled 16,529,800 metric tons. Included in the total were coal, oil fuel, metals for munitions, chemicals for explosives, and substantial amounts of rubber and timber for a multitude of other war purposes.

Ciano estimated that this would take up 17,000 train loads. And Mussolini added a footnote of his own to this prodigious bill: "If these deliveries cannot be guaranteed, it is my duty to tell you that the sacrifices for which I would ask the Italian people could all be in vain, and that in pursuing my own affairs I might compromise yours."

Attolico added to the confusion by making a premeditated *gaffe*. Asked how soon Italy would expect the delivery of these supplies, he told Ribbentrop: "Right

Could Hitler have been bought off?

Between July 18 and 21, 1939, Herr Wohltat, an official in Göring's financial administration, was in London for a conference on whaling. During this period he was approached by Sir Horace Wilson, head of the British Civil Service, who, Wohltat claimed, led him to believe that the proposal he was about to make had the sanction of the Prime Minister.

The proposal was simple: if Germany would give up her hostile attitude to Poland, Britain would make available to her a loan of up to £1,000 million to cover the costs of disarmament, which was also insisted upon.

This was outside Wohltat's competence and he returned to Germany for further instructions. Nothing more was ever heard of the matter, and it seems unlikely that Hitler was even informed of the offer.

way. Before hostilities begin." This earned him a disagreeable reply from Ribbentrop, but it was part of Mussolini's desire to get his personal declaration of insolvency counter-signed by Hitler himself.

This was done in a letter dated August 26, which Ribbentrop read over the telephone to Mackensen in Rome the same day. It declared that Hitler would supply the amounts of timber, coal, steel, and potassium carbonate for which Mussolini had asked. But he could offer only 30 anti-aircraft batteries instead of the 150 which had been requested, and none of the other materials. The letter was couched in the most friendly terms. "In these circumstances," it concluded, "I understand your position, Duce, and I ask you to contribute nothing more than active propaganda and appropriate military demonstrations to the action which I have in mind to contain the English and French forces."

The Reich would benefit, more than anything else, from the silence which until the last minute Italy was to maintain with regard to her intention of limiting herself to a policy of "non-belligerence". Hitler hoped that doubts about Italy's position would prevent Britain and France from rapid counter-moves. But this policy amounted to making Italy the lightning-conductor in this diplomatic atmosphere which crackled with electricity – a rôle which, surreptitiously, Italy would refuse to play. And, despite Hitler's hopes to the contrary, all these fluctuations in Italian policy were known in Paris and London.

Stern warning from Chamberlain

Hitler had calculated that the news of the Moscow pact would make Chamberlain, with his preference for peace, drop any further idea of going to war. But even before Ribbentrop had got back from Moscow to Berlin, a personal note from the Prime Minister to the Führer arrived at the Berghof – and dispelled all remaining doubts, stating that Britain would give military aid to Poland in the event of German aggression.

If the German leaders in 1939 thought little of France, they gave much more thought to England. "Corporal Hitler" himself, a veteran of the Western Front in World War I, respected the cold tenacity of the British and their willingness to fight on until final victory was won. He could not shrug off the conclusion of Chamberlain's letter: "It would be a dangerous illusion to think that a war, once begun, could be brought to a rapid end, even if success were won on one of the many fronts to which it would spread."

Hitler's main concern now was to neutralise the British, who, he believed, had persuaded the French to model their attitude on that of London. As Hitler and Ribbentrop saw it, Britain was the prime mover of the Western coalition. Paris, without enthusiasm, certainly, had echoed the bellicose attitude of the British; but Paris would return to a pacifist outlook if the British could be persuaded to do the same. According to the British *Blue Book*, the Germans "were constantly looking for a way to make the Anglo-Polish alliance

△ △ *German "Reich War Day" poster, June 1939.* △ *Ominous reminder of the 25th anniversary of Hindenburg's great victory over the Russians at Tannenberg in late August 1914.*

△ *"Germany will never be encircled!" bellows a world-hungry Hitler in this* Punch *cartoon by E. H. Shepherd.*

△ *A resigned note from* Le Journal *of Paris: "Lord, Lord, you must re-make the world; you made it too small for the dictators."*

break up. On August 24, Göring told the Polish Ambassador in Berlin, Lipski, that the hurdle between their two countries was not Danzig but the alliance with Great Britain." On August 25, therefore, Hitler received the British Ambassador in Berlin, Sir Nevile Henderson, and spoke to him along the following lines:

Nothing the Prime Minister could say could cause the least modification to the claims of the Reich on Danzig and the Corridor. If war should result from Mr. Chamberlain's words, however, Germany would be in a much more advantageous position than 1914, for she would not have to fight on two fronts. But was war between Britain and Germany unavoidable? If Britain would consent to stay at peace, Hitler was prepared to guarantee the security of the whole of the British Empire, and would offer co-operation "wherever in the world such co-operation might be necessary". On August 25, also, Hitler received Coulondre again and blamed the break in Franco-German relations on France. On the next day, Daladier sent Hitler a conciliatory letter, but the German Führer had gone too far for conciliation.

Hitler plays for time

Here, then, was a third reason for the postponement of the attack on Poland, after the news of the Anglo-Polish alliance and Attolico's message that Italy's programme must be one of "non-belligerence". Now Hitler knew that he could not open hostilities until he had received the British Government's reply to these, his latest proposals.

The British Ambassador was given the use of a German aircraft to take these proposals in person to London, where he arrived on the morning of August 26. By the evening of the 28th he was back at the New Chancellery with Chamberlain's reply. The offer of German protection for the British Empire had – not surprisingly – failed. "In no case can the British Government, in return for an advantage offered to Great Britain, agree to a settlement which would jeopardise the independence of a State to which it has given its firm guarantee."

Hoping that an "equitable" solution could be reached over the differences between Germany and Poland, Chamberlain suggested that "the next step should

be the opening of direct negotiations between the German and Polish Governments", in respect of which he had already received "certain assurances from the Polish Government". If such negotiations could arrive at a settlement, this would "open the door to world-wide peace"; but failure to do so would put an end to all hopes of an understanding between Great Britain and Germany. What was more, it would precipitate first the two countries and then the whole world into war. This would be a tragedy without parallel in history.

Hitler now knew that there were no hopes of winning over the British, but he still had a faint chance of localising the conflict. He had the time to convince the German people that he had done everything in his power to avoid bloodshed. He also had to give some satisfaction to the appeals for peace which were flooding in from Washington, from numerous neutral states, and from the Vatican.

On August 29, Hitler received Henderson and told him: "In these circumstances, the German Government agrees to accept the British Government's offer of their good services in securing the despatch to Berlin of a Polish Emissary with full powers. They count on the arrival of this Emissary on Wednesday, August 30."

Hitler ignored Henderson's objections that this left far too little time for a Polish envoy to arrive in Berlin for negotiations. But was it really a question of negotiation? Hitler's attitude implied that he was prepared to talk with a one-man surrender deputation – with or without a white flag – who would be ready to sign a document defining Germany's terms for Danzig and the Corridor. In any case, Hitler never dreamed that Warsaw would find his request acceptable. According to Halder, Hitler had set the following timetable on August 29:

"August 30: Polish envoy arrives in Berlin.
August 31: Rupture [*zerplatzen*] with Poland.
September 1: Resort to force."

Slanging match with Ribbentrop

The interview between Ribbentrop and Henderson at midnight August 30, just before the deadline laid down by Hitler for the arrival of a Polish envoy, was one of the stormiest encounters in the relations between the Western democracies and the Reich, and shows Hitler's completely shameless determination to make the breach at all costs.

Henderson began by stating that it was unreasonable to expect the British Government to arrange for the arrival of a Polish envoy on 24 hours' notice. "The time is up," replied Ribbentrop icily; "Where is the Polish envoy?" Henderson began to lose control. His face reddened and his hands began to shake as he started to read the official British reply to Hitler's request that Britain and Poland should refrain from aggressive troop movements. "What unheard-of impudence!" Ribbentrop interrupted furiously, and, crossing his arms on his chest, added provocatively: "Have you anything else to say?" "That the Germans are committing acts of sabotage in Poland!" "That is an abominable lie!" shouted Ribbentrop in a rage; "All I have to tell you is that the situation is damned serious!" Henderson could take no more. Stabbing a finger at Ribbentrop, he shouted: "*Damned serious*, you say? That is not how responsible statesmen talk!" Ribbentrop leaped out of his chair. "What did you say?" he shouted. Henderson also jumped up, and the two diplomats faced each other like fighting cocks. But their fury passed; they controlled themselves,

and sat down again. Ribbentrop pulled out of his pocket a sheet of paper which contained a proposal for the settlement of the Polish problem. He read it carefully, taking his time. Then the blow fell. Henderson asked that he be given the text of this document to pass it on to his government – a perfectly reasonable request. "I could hardly believe my ears," recalled Schmidt, the interpreter, "when Ribbentrop replied with a taut smile: 'No, I cannot give you these proposals.' And he threw the paper on the table, saying: 'In any case, it is too late: the Polish envoy has not come.'"

"I suddenly realised," Schmidt continued, "what sort of game Hitler and Ribbentrop were actually playing. At this moment – midnight, August 30 – it was clear to me that their proposition was nothing but a lure and could never have come to anything. At any price the Poles must not know about it, for they might accept! All I could do was to draw a thick red line across the notes I was taking of Ribbentrop's statements – a line which marked the transition-point when the decision for peace or war was taken."

△ *Heated words fly between British Ambassador Henderson and Ribbentrop in Berlin. At one moment it seemed that they would actually come to blows.*
◁ *The last hours of peace: Polish Ambassador Lipski leaves the New Chancellery on the afternoon of August 31, having just heard Ribbentrop's contemptuous statement that further discussions between Poland and Germany are pointless. The Wehrmacht has already been given its marching orders for dawn on the following day – September 1, 1939.*

Disciples and Leader.

The order goes out

The following day, at 1830 hours, Ambassador Lipski called on Ribbentrop to inform him that the Polish Government had accepted the British suggestion for direct discussion between Warsaw and Berlin. All Ribbentrop asked him was:

"Do you have full powers to treat with us?"

"No," replied Lipski.

"Then," Ribbentrop concluded, "It is completely useless for us to discuss the matter further." The last effort towards maintaining world peace came from Mussolini at 1200 hours on the next day, when he proposed that France, Great Britain, Germany, Italy, and Poland get together around a conference table. It was too late. Hitler had decided to go to war.

But already, at 1700 hours on the 31st, General Gerd von Rundstedt, commanding Army Group South on the Neisse and who was to lead the main offensive against Poland, had received the signal which would unleash the attack at dawn on the following day: "Y=1.9.0445".

CHAPTER 7
No Help from the Allies

The German invasion of Poland was launched without the Polish Ambassador in Berlin hearing Hitler's latest proposals for a peaceful solution to the problem of Danzig and the Corridor. But it is obvious that these "proposals" had only been drawn up for the purpose of playing to the gallery of world opinion and misleading the German public about the true nature of the "negotiations". Apart from this, the German attack went in while Italy was submitting to Paris and London the suggestion for a five-power conference that was to meet on September 5 and "examine the clauses in the Treaty of Versailles which are at the root of the trouble".

In taking the step of launching the invasion, Hitler was gambling that the Western powers would not be able to give Poland any rapid or effective aid. He was right – but he had drawn the wrong conclusion about the sincerity of the British and French reaction to his resort to force.

On Friday, September 1, on hearing that the armed forces of the Reich had attacked Poland, Britain and France proclaimed general mobilisation and

Luftwaffe readiness: warming up a Messerschmitt Bf 110 fighter.

neutrality, at least of non-belligerence. In so doing, Ciano acted with prudence, for there were many exiled Italians in Paris and London who urged France and Britain to issue Mussolini with an ultimatum, calling upon him to open Italian territory to the British and French forces, or even to put his fleet at their disposal.

Great Britain declared war on Germany at 1100 hours on Sunday, September 3, on the expiry of her ultimatum presented two hours earlier. At noon, the French Ambassador in Berlin called on Ribbentrop, and on receiving Germany's refusal to suspend operations against Poland, informed the German Foreign Minister that a state of war would exist between France and Germany as from 1700 hours.

The time lag between these two declarations of war caused some dissension in Paris and London. The British Admiralty pressed for an early opening of hostilities, so that British warships might be able to intercept Germany's merchant shipping while it was still at sea and to prevent her submarines from escaping from the North Sea. On the other hand, the French Army High Command asked for sufficient time to complete the first phases of mobilisation without the threat of German air attack. But Daladier put pressure on the General Staff, and succeeded in getting the declaration of war, originally fixed for 2100 hours on the 4th, brought back to 1700 hours, September 3.

By then the Polish Army had already been in battle for 60 hours and 30 minutes . . .

▷▷ *Panzer punch: a Pzkw I copes with a wall in short order.*
△ *Polish officer cadets of 1939. Soon many of these new officers would be charging German tanks with cold steel in their futile attempt to defend the Danzig "Corridor".*
▷ *British comment in the late summer of 1939. It would be months before Britain could even begin to match the contributions of her Allies in terms of land forces – a fact which caused much bitterness.*

charged their Ambassadors in Berlin with delivering identical messages to the German Foreign Ministry: Germany must halt her invasion of Poland and withdraw her troops from Polish territory immediately. If she did not, Britain and France would "fulfil their obligations to Poland without hesitation".

The withdrawal of the German troops was seen as the essential preliminary to the five-power conference suggested by Mussolini. But the demand for this withdrawal, reasonable though it was, caused Mussolini to abandon the idea – and in fact it is difficult to see how he could have recommended such a solution to Hitler. Despite Hitler's express wishes, however, Ciano took it upon himself to inform the British and French Ambassadors in Rome that Italy would keep to a policy, if not of

"HALF A MO'
HITLER.
LET'S HAVE OUR
HOLIDAYS FIRST"

AHM 921

△ "Flying artillery" of the Luftwaffe–Junkers Ju 87 dive-bombers. The famous word "Stuka", commonly used to describe these aircraft, was in fact an overall label for dive-bombing aircraft, being derived from the correct term Sturzkampfflugzeug. Formed into special dive-bombing units, the Stuka crews soon acquired a deadly accuracy which made them indispensable to the ground forces. Events would prove that they were just as accurate when attacking Allied shipping. ◁ German anti-aircraft crew. "Flak"–Fliegerabwehrkanone–was another vital weapon in the Wehrmacht's armoury. Advancing army units were lavishly equipped with flak guns which could make a recently-captured position safe from air attack within minutes. The German anti-aircraft arm was organised as a separate branch of the Luftwaffe.

Balance of forces, September 1939

What were the main strengths and weaknesses of the two sides when World War II began? How, if at all, could the Allies have helped Poland?

The Allies had an enormous naval superiority. Admittedly, the British and French warships were weak in anti-aircraft defence, as the German dive-bombers were to prove during the battle for Norway in 1940. But with 676 ships (built or launched) against 130, the Allies clearly had the upper hand at sea. Their position was strengthened by the fact that the pressing needs of German war production forced Grand-Admiral Raeder to abandon the "Z-Plan" programme of heavy warship construction; even the two German aircraft-carriers—one of which, the *Graf Zeppelin*, had already been launched—could not be completed.

Germany had 57 U-boats, under the command of Commodore Karl Dönitz, 32 of them small boats designed for coastal operations (Types I and II). They could challenge the Allied control of the North Sea but were totally unsuitable for Atlantic commerce-raiding. This, however, was not all: within a few weeks, Dönitz was to learn that his U-boats suffered from glaring technical faults in their torpedoes.

On the other side of the ledger, the Luftwaffe was supreme in the air. On the first day of war, its order of battle totalled some 4,700 aircraft (including 552 three-engined Junkers Ju 52 transports). The anti-aircraft defences of the Reich, and the German mobile A.A. forces in the field, were the best in Europe, totalling over 9,000 guns. Of these, 2,600 were heavy-calibre weapons (8.8-cm and 10.5-cm).

But the Luftwaffe's trump card in the Polish campaign was its nine dive-bomber units flying the Junkers Ju 87 Stuka. (The notorious word "Stuka" is an abbreviation of the German "*Sturzkampfflugzeug*", or dive-bombing aircraft.) These gave the Wehrmacht a reserve of "flying artillery", which could be called in to deliver pinpoint bombing attacks at crucial moments in the offensive. Thoroughly trained in co-operation with the armoured and motorised units of the army, the Stukas gave the latter every opportunity to use their manoeuvrability and speed to the full without getting tied down in set-piece attacks which called for traditional artillery support.

In the Allied camp, the Polish Air Force, totalling 842 aircraft, was weak and obsolescent. France had virtually no modern bombers which could be pitted against the German fighter and A.A. defences. The Royal Air Force totalled 3,600 aircraft, of which a large proportion was totally obsolete; the R.A.F. also had to reserve many aircraft for duties outside Europe.

There were absolutely no plans for co-operation between the French and British air forces except for a mutual agreement not to bomb German territory—for fear of massive reprisals against either of their two nations. In any case, the resources of R.A.F. Bomber Command were so puny that they would have been capable of inflicting only pinpricks on Germany during the autumn of 1939.

There was also no agreement in the Allied High Command, and personal

▽ *French armour: a Renault R-35 tank. The R-35 appeared in 1935 and was adopted as an infantry support vehicle – a rôle which in itself was years behind the German ideas on the correct use of tanks on the battlefield. The R-35 had other significant weaknesses: no radio, a top speed of around 12 mph, an over-worked commander-gunner; it was under-powered and its short 37-mm gun was of World War I vintage.*

△ *The watch on the Rhine:*
German troops amid the
"dragon's teeth" anti-tank
defences of the Siegfried Line or
Westwall.
▷ *Garrison troops in the*
Siegfried Line parade before the
Reich War Flag to hear an
address from their commander.

rivalries, normally camouflaged by official courtesy, undermined planning for joint operations. The French journalist "Pertinax" noted one example in 1940: "In the meeting on April 3 General Weygand delivered a long monologue. He wished to create a Balkan front, estimating that the hundred-odd divisions scattered throughout the Balkan states friendly to the Allies could be concentrated under French leadership. While Weygand was reading this memorandum, Daladier muttered and shrugged his shoulders. Gamelin did not say a word, but merely raised his eyes to heaven. All this struck him as dangerous and absurd. Afterwards, in private, he explained: 'Obviously, it would be desirable to make Germany fight on several fronts. But the time for the Western offensive will soon be here . . .' "

As far as the land forces were concern-

ed, the total manpower strengths meant nothing until the differing processes of mobilisation had been completed, by which time it was too late to help Poland.

Thanks to Hitler's retention of the political initiative, the Wehrmacht was better prepared than its opponents to jump off at 0430 hours on September 1. But general mobilisation in Poland had not been proclaimed until 1100 hours the day before, while mobilisation in France, ordered on the first news of the German invasion of Poland, did not get under way until September 2. The result was that Marshal Edward Rydz-Smigly, the Polish Commander-in-Chief, never had all the resources that would have made his plan for concentration work, and that by the time that General Gamelin had completed his own preparations, Poland had already received her death-blow.

△ "War is action; chatter is treason"–a hard-hitting German variation on the "careless talk costs lives" theme.

△ *Call-up in France: mobilisation posters call the French reservists to the colours in 1939. French mobilisation was on a far greater scale than in Britain, touching one man in eight of the population. The British call-up only reached one man in 48.*
▽ *British counterpart: Nelson's Column is pressed into service as a recruiting hoarding.*

The Panzer élite

Every one of the 53 German first line divisions in the field had modern arms and equipment. This was not the case with the 28 French divisions, recruited at the same time, assigned to the North-East Front in France. And in the Polish Army, most of the available weapons were obsolescent, a large part of them dating from the 1920's or even earlier. In the Wehrmacht, the larger formations did have certain weaknesses in their armament, especially in artillery. But in the French Army matters were far worse, particularly in the "Category B" reserve divisions, which had been mobilised with grave deficiencies in every sphere.

The biggest contrast of all was in the motorised and armoured divisions of either side. True, the French Army had seven motorised divisions while the German Army had only four, with a fifth made up of the 23,000 men of the *Waffen-S.S.* (military S.S.). But General Maurice Gamelin's order of battle had nothing to match the six German *Panzer* or armoured divisions. Nor did the two French light mechanised divisions come up to the standard of the four *Leichte Divisionen* of the Wehrmacht.

The French concentrated on forming brigades equipped with modern heavy tanks, but as they could not be given adequate air cover, Gamelin refused to group the existing brigades into divisions, although he was in the process of raising armoured divisions from scratch. In the German Army, on the other hand, the Panzer division was merely the basic unit, two of them being combined to make an armoured corps. When the Polish campaign began, Generals Heinz Guderian, Erich Hoeppner, Hermann Hoth, Ewald von Kleist, and Gustav von Wietersheim soon showed their skill in commanding and manoeuvring such corps of armour.

So much for the deficiencies of the French Army in organisation and equipment. Both would bear disastrous fruits in the months to come. But what of its manpower, its morale? Was the French Army lacking in offensive spirit? And do the operations of 1939 deserve the description given to them by Colonel A. Goutard in his excellent study of the 1940 campaign as "the war of lost opportunities"?

In his memoirs, published in 1963, ex-Prime Minister Paul Reynaud condemned Gamelin's half-hearted strategy, quoting the statements made at Nuremberg after the war by members of the German High Command. General Alfred Jodl's opinion was: "In 1939 catastrophe [the continuation of the war] was not averted because 110 French and British divisions did not attack our 25 divisions in the West." General Keitel, too, was quoted as saying: "We were surprised that France did not attack Germany during the Polish campaign. Any form of attack would have shaken our screen of 25 reserve divisions and could only have encountered feeble resistance."

Why did France not attack in the West?

The figures quoted by Jodl and Keitel are, however, wrong. On September 1, 1939, the German Army Group "C", commanded by Colonel-General Wilhelm Ritter von Leeb, held the front between Basle and Aix-la-Chapelle. It was not made up of 25 divisions but of 34, to which was added two-thirds of the 22nd Airborne Division. The group was also reinforced after the news came in that France and Britain were at war with Germany: the Army High Command (O.K.H., for *Oberkommando des Heeres*) decided to add nine reserve divisions to the Western Front armies. These divisions completed their move by September 10, so that Leeb's strength on the next day totalled $43\frac{2}{3}$ divisions.

Similarly, the French forces facing Leeb were much weaker than Jodl and Keitel claimed at Nuremberg. For a start, there were no British forces at all until the I Corps took up its place in the line, at Lille, on October 3 – a full month after Britain's declaration of war. Nor were there anything like 110 Allied divisions on the Western Front.

The decree of mobilisation gave Gamelin 81 infantry (seven of them motorised), three cavalry, and two light mechanised divisions, excluding the 13 garrison divisions of the Maginot Line. This immediately brings down Jodl's and Keitel's overall figure from 110 to 86 divisions. But even this is misleading, for Gamelin had to cover the Italian and Spanish frontiers as well as the Western Front.

At the time of France's declaration of war, the French Army in the field totalled 30 infantry divisions. Fourteen of these

were in North Africa, manning the French "Mareth Line" defences and keeping an eye on Italian concentrations in Libya. Nine others were deployed on the Alpine front. Seven were available for the Western Front, and there were a few battalions of Pyrenean *chasseurs*, mountain troops, screening the Spanish frontier.

The acute shortage of manpower was not helped by the fact that mobilisation and concentration was no faster in 1939 than it had been in 1914. It took three weeks. Not until September 20 were the last units in position. Under these conditions how could Gamelin have launched a rapid attack on the Germans in the West while Polish resistance continued? Adding the manpower of the Maginot Line, Gamelin by now had a total of 57 divisions – 52 infantry, three cavalry, and two light mechanised divisions – deployed between Belfort and Maubeuge. Of these, 31 were earmarked for operations in the Saar between September 1 and 12.

The French Army: geared to the defensive

Gamelin's army lacked not only the wherewithal to attack: it had also never been intended that the French Army should be prepared for an immediate offensive.

Since June 1932, the fortunes of France and of her army had been supervised by a succession of 19 governments, eight war ministers, and eight ministers of finance. This was bad enough, but the roots of the trouble ran even deeper. In 1925, Paul Painlevé, the War Minister, had laid down that the ideal rôle of the French Army should be "to achieve a rational system of national defence, adequate in times of danger but unsuited to adventures and conquests".

This made the French Army essentially reservist and defensive in character, and also meant that the preparation of the French war machine would be a slow process.

It is interesting to note that all this was not lost on the Polish High Command, and that Warsaw did everything that it could to mitigate the consequences. After the fall of Warsaw in September 1939, General von Manstein, Chief-of-Staff of the German Army Group "South", had access to the Polish Army archives and unearthed some fascinating material. In the first months of 1938, General Kutrzeba, the Director of the Polish Military Academy, had submitted his views on the defence of the nation to Marshal Rydz-Smigly. Kutrzeba's personal opinion was a sound one: he held that "it will be necessary to wait for help from France; Poland will have to rely on her own forces for six to eight weeks, even if the French react promptly."

△ Flammenwerfer! *A German assault pioneer tests his flame-thrower on an exercise.*
▽ *Backbone of the German Army: the infantryman. He had the unglamorous job of smashing enemy units encircled by the Panzer divisions and then following on in the dust of the armoured cars and tanks.*

△ *French heavy artillery crew prepares to support the abortive Saar offensive, France's "contribution" during the Polish campaign. Prételat's troops shuffled cautiously forward to the Siegfried Line—and stopped. Afterwards, one French commander told a British correspondent, "It was simply a token invasion," and added: "Now that the Polish question is liquidated we have gone back to our lines. What else did you expect?"*

Poland knew that France could not help in time

The following year the same question was the subject of a 48-hour series of talks between General Gamelin and General Kasprzycki, the Polish War Minister, on May 16–17. A protocol emerged, containing the following points:

"As soon as part of the French forces is available (about the 3rd day after France's general mobilisation), France will launch a series of progressive offensives with limited objectives.

"As soon as the main German attacks come to bear on Poland, France will launch an offensive with the bulk of her forces (not earlier than the 15th day after France's mobilisation)."

General Joseph Georges, commanding the French North-East Front, intervened in the discussion to give "some information on the Siegfried Line and on the artillery that will be needed to attack it". His estimate was that "to attack this line and achieve a breakthrough cannot be contemplated until the 17th day [after

mobilisation]".

Gamelin then declared that three-quarters of the French Army could—before any operations were launched on the North-East Front—undertake an offensive between the Rhine and the Moselle on the 15th day after mobilisation. But as far as the actual course of events in the Polish campaign was concerned, this meant the day before Soviet Russia stabbed Poland in the back and attacked from the East . . .

The relevant documents do not show that the Polish War Minister raised any objection to Gamelin's programme. From this one can only conclude that Marshal Rydz-Smigly and the majority of his French colleagues had absolutely no conception of the paralysing effects of dive-bombing attacks or of the imaginative use of armoured forces. (This, to be fair, applied to many German commanders.)

In addition to this paradoxical situation there was the incredible optimism of Gamelin himself. Pierre-Etienne Flandin recalled: "I met Gamelin on August 27. He spoke in the most optimistic terms about the Polish forces. When I pointed out that [the Germans] had expressed their belief that they could crush Poland in three weeks, Gamelin rebuked me for believing Hitler's predictions. 'I know the Polish Army perfectly,' he said. 'Its troops are excellent and its commanders beyond praise. The Poles will hold out and we will lose no time in coming to their aid.' And when I remained sceptical and asked how we could help the Poles, he replied with great conviction: 'The Poles will hold out for at least six months and we will come to their aid via Rumania.' I left the War Ministry, horror-stricken."

France's attack: stopped in its tracks

Operation "Saar", the plans for which were contained in a French Army Instruction of July 24, 1939, was the first of the limited offensives mentioned by Gamelin. It was directed by General Gaston Prételat, commander of the French 2nd Army Group. The attack went in on September 7, and was a complete fiasco.

Everything was against the French. For a start, the sector of the frontier between the Rhine and the Moselle selected for the French attack had been

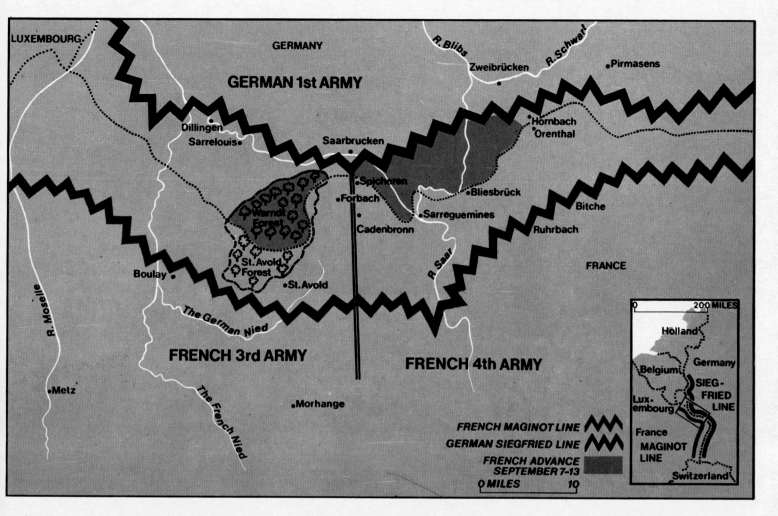

Map labels:

LUXEMBOURG.
GERMANY
R. Blibs
R. Schwarz
Zweibrücken
•Pirmasens
GERMAN 1st ARMY
Dillingen
Sarrelouis•
Hornbach
Orenthal
Saarbrucken
•Spicheren
•Bliesbrück
•Forbach
Warndt Forest
Sarreguemines
Bitche
Cadenbronn
Ruhrbach
St. Avold Forest
FRANCE
Boulay •
•St.Avold
R. Moselle
The German Nied
FRENCH 3rd ARMY
FRENCH 4th ARMY
•Metz
The French Nied
•Morhange

Holland
Belgium
Germany
SIEG-
FRIED
LINE
Lux-
embourg
France
MAGINOT
LINE
Switzerland
0   200 MILES

FRENCH MAGINOT LINE
GERMAN SIEGFRIED LINE
FRENCH ADVANCE
SEPTEMBER 7-13
0 MILES   10

defined by the victors of Waterloo in 1815 with the express purpose of making French aggression difficult. Thus in 1939 the Germans held all the high ground. German-held salients also extended into French territory, and these would have to be reduced before the Siegfried Line proper could be assaulted. In addition to this, the Siegfried Line was sufficiently far behind the German front line to compel the French to bring their own artillery (if it was to be within range of the casemates of the Line) within range of German counter-battery fire.

After patrolling operations, Prételat launched his attack on September 7, but it hardly got past its start-lines. A total of 31 divisions had been put at Prételat's disposal, including 14 first-line units, but only nine were used eventually. General Edouard Réquin's 4th Army, with its right flank in the Bitche region and its left on the Saar, managed to capture seven and a half miles of German territory, while its neighbour, General Condé's 3rd Army, pinched out the heavily-wooded Warndt Forest salient.

Commanding the German 1st Army, General Erwin von Witzleben had 17 divisions to meet this attack, and ten of these had been recruited only recently. But his troops made skilful use of their advantage in terrain, relying heavily on cleverly-sited anti-tank and anti-personnel minefields. The French were unfamiliar with this threat and possessed no mine detectors. Houses booby-trapped with explosives added to the German minefield defences.

What of the Siegfried Line itself, which the French had planned to attack after September 17. General Siegfried Westphal has gone on record as describing the Line as a "gigantic bluff", but it was not. Its defences were sound, and the French artillery could do little damage to them. Major-General Ulrich Liss, head of "Section West" of German Army Intelligence, stated that the French 155-mm shells caused negligible damage. The heavier 220-mm and 280-mm guns were not provided with delayed-action fused shells, which would have enabled the projectiles to penetrate the casemates before exploding. Liss admitted that the French guns maintained a high and accurate rate of fire, but stated that a large number of the French shells failed to explode as they came from stocks dating back to World War I.

△ *The negligible French gains during the Saar offensive: two insignificant snippets of terrain which the Germans had evacuated anyway. The western defences of the Reich were not even dented.*

▽ *"Drôle de guerre" – troops of a Maginot Line fortress while away the time playing cards. As the months of inactivity went by, indolence and drink steadily eroded the French soldier's morale.*

German Messerschmitt Bf 110C

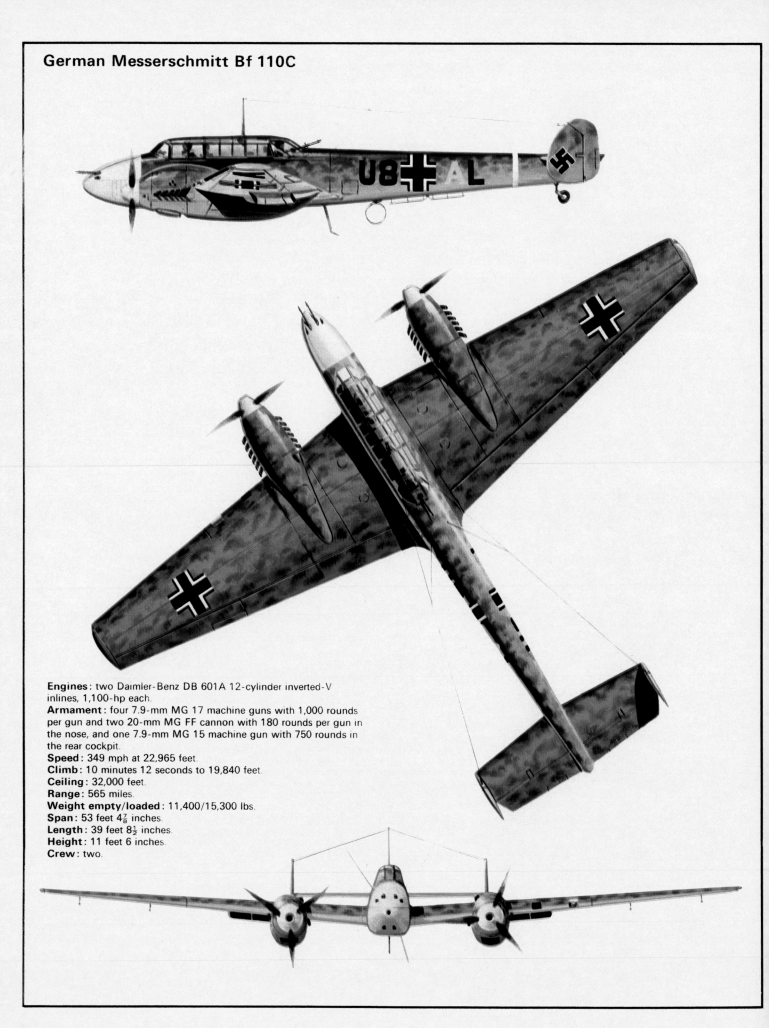

Engines: two Daimler-Benz DB 601A 12-cylinder inverted-V inlines, 1,100-hp each.

Armament: four 7.9-mm MG 17 machine guns with 1,000 rounds per gun and two 20-mm MG FF cannon with 180 rounds per gun in the nose, and one 7.9-mm MG 15 machine gun with 750 rounds in the rear cockpit.

Speed: 349 mph at 22,965 feet.

Climb: 10 minutes 12 seconds to 19,840 feet.

Ceiling: 32,000 feet.

Range: 565 miles.

Weight empty/loaded: 11,400/15,300 lbs.

Span: 53 feet $4\frac{7}{8}$ inches.

Length: 39 feet $8\frac{1}{2}$ inches.

Height: 11 feet 6 inches.

Crew: two.

From the moment that the German campaign against Poland started in the early morning of September 1, 1939, there was no hope that the Poles could stem the *Blitzkrieg*. The German tanks moved forward inexorably, with the well-trained Ju 87 Stuka units providing the equivalent of highly mobile artillery for them. Whenever a Polish strongpoint or concentration was detected, the Stukas were called in to destroy these actual or potential threats to the German advance.

Arriving over the target, the Stukas would peel off from their unit one by one to plummet down, the air-brakes under their wings holding the dive-speed down to that which would make the aircraft most stable for bomb-dropping. As the bomb hurtled towards the ground from a few hundred feet up, the Stuka would pull out of its dive and climb up to join the rest of its unit.

The only Polish aircraft with even the slightest chance of dealing with the Stukas was the *Panstwowe Zaklady Lotnicze* (P.Z.L. or State Aircraft Factory) built P-11 fighters. But these were obsolescent and only available in small numbers, and for all the courage and determination of the pilots, there was little that this small force could achieve.

The task of the P.Z.L. P-11's was in itself difficult enough, but it was rendered almost completely impossible in the face of overwhelming German fighter superiority—and this superiority was both qualitative and quantitative. Roaming far behind the lines were large numbers of two-engined Messerschmitt Bf 110 long-range fighters, ready to pounce on any Polish aircraft which might appear confident of safety in their own rear area airfields. The Bf 110 *Zerstörer* (Destroyer) had a considerable speed advantage over its Polish opponents, and also carried a particularly formidable armament.

This is, of course, only one small part of the story of the Luftwaffe's crushing of the Polish Air Force, relating in general terms to the three aircraft illustrated here. There were naturally other aircraft involved in the fighting, especially the P.Z.L. P-23 *Karaś* (Carp) light bomber and reconnaissance aircraft on the Polish side, and the Messerschmitt Bf 109 single-seat fighter, and the Heinkel He 111 and Dornier Do 17 medium bombers on the German.

Polish aircraft losses in operations between September 1 and September 17 totalled 333. Of the remaining strength of the Polish Air Force, 116 machines of all types were flown into Rumania and there interned.

As we have seen, numerically the most important fighter in service with the Polish *Lotnictwo Wojskowe* (Military Aviation) was the P.Z.L. P-11 *Jedenastka* (p. 98). This type had first flown in 1931, and was a development of the P-7 of the late 1920's. The most distinctive feature of the series was the shoulder-mounted, braced gull-wing, the design of Zygmunt Pulawski, who was killed in an air crash on March 31, 1931.

When first introduced, the design was very advanced, providing much of the strength of a biplane planform with the reduced drag of a monoplane. Despite this, the design was obsolete in 1939 in comparison with the latest low-wing monoplanes in production for the air forces of Great Britain, France, Germany, and the United States. A further development, the P-24, was about to enter service with the Polish Air Force in September 1939.

Though outclassed in speed, the P.Z.L. P-11 achieved a small measure of success by possessing excellent visibility, great agility, and considerable ruggedness. Thirty P-7's and 129 P-11's were in service at the opening of hostilities. The aircraft illustrated, a P-11c, belonged to 161 Squadron, the "Turkeys", of the 6th Air Regiment at L'vov, attached to the Border Protection Corps.

The Junkers Ju 87 (p. 99) proved to be the Luftwaffe's trump card in the Polish campaign. The type had first flown in 1936 with twin fins and rudders at the ends of the tailplane, large "trousers" round the undercarriage, and a British Rolls-Royce Kestrel engine. The design was soon modified to a single fin and rudder, and the first Ju 87A's entered service in 1937.

Three were sent to Spain for operational testing, and proved remarkably successful, being able to deliver their bombs with an accuracy never before achieved.

The model illustrated here, the Ju 87B, went into production in the middle of 1938, not being superseded on the production lines by the 87D until 1940. The 87B differed from earlier models in having an uprated engine, offering 50 per cent more power, "spats" instead of "trousers" for the undercarriage, and a much improved cockpit canopy, which gave the crew very good visibility. Altogether, some 5,000 Ju 87's were built up to the time the type was discontinued in 1944, when it was completely obsolete. With the declining ability to undertake its designed dive-bombing rôle, later marks of the Ju 87 were rearmed with heavy cannon and used as anti-tank aircraft.

Operationally, the Ju 87 was remarkably successful in Poland, less so in France, and a complete disaster in the Battle of Britain. Its success in the following years of the war was directly proportional to the absence of good fighter opposition. The reason is simple: basically, the Ju 87 was a slow, cumbersome, and poorly-protected machine, and could not survive in the same skies as efficiently-flown fighters. It also proved very vulnerable to ground fire, in the rear fuselage where all the control cables were grouped closely together.

The accompanying illustration is of a Ju 87B-1, aircraft "C" of the 1 *Staffel* (in the I *Gruppe*) of *Stukageschwader* 77.

The Messerschmitt Bf 110 twin-engined fighter (p. 96) was typical of the family of such long-range escort machines designed in Britain, France, Germany, Holland, and Japan in the middle and late 1930's. The idea behind the design was to provide protection for the bombers which contemporary strategic air theory thought would be the arbiters of the next war.

The prototype flew for the first time in May 1936, but by the time the engines intended for the type had been brought to the required degree of reliability, the 110 was too late to join the other German types being tested in Spain. Deliveries of the first production model, the 110C, began in the spring of 1939. The type was successful in the first year of the war, but its disadvantages were brought plainly to light in the Battle of Britain. The chief of these proved to be its lack of manoeuvrability, which made it very susceptible to attack from nimbler single-seaters.

Nevertheless, the 110 remained in service throughout the war, something over 6,000 examples being built before the defeat of Germany. The type proved itself to be very versatile (as a bomber, ground attack, reconnaissance, and night fighter aircraft), especially in the last rôle, that of night fighter, in which it was the most successful design of the war.

Even though the original purpose for which the 110 (and several of its contemporaries) had been designed had proved to be misguided, the Bf 110 can be regarded as one of the war's more successful and versatile designs, despite the scorn which has been heaped upon it from many quarters.

The aircraft illustrated is a Bf 110C-4, aircraft "A" of the 3 *Staffel* (which was part of the I *Gruppe*) in *Zerstörergeschwader* 26 "Horst Wessel". (A *Geschwader* or group normally had three *Gruppen* or wings, numbered I, II and III, each made up of three *Staffeln* or squadrons. *Staffeln* 1, 2, and 3 belonged to I *Gruppe*, 4, 5, and 6 to II *Gruppe*, and so on.)

The Air Battle for Poland

Polish P.Z.L. P-11c

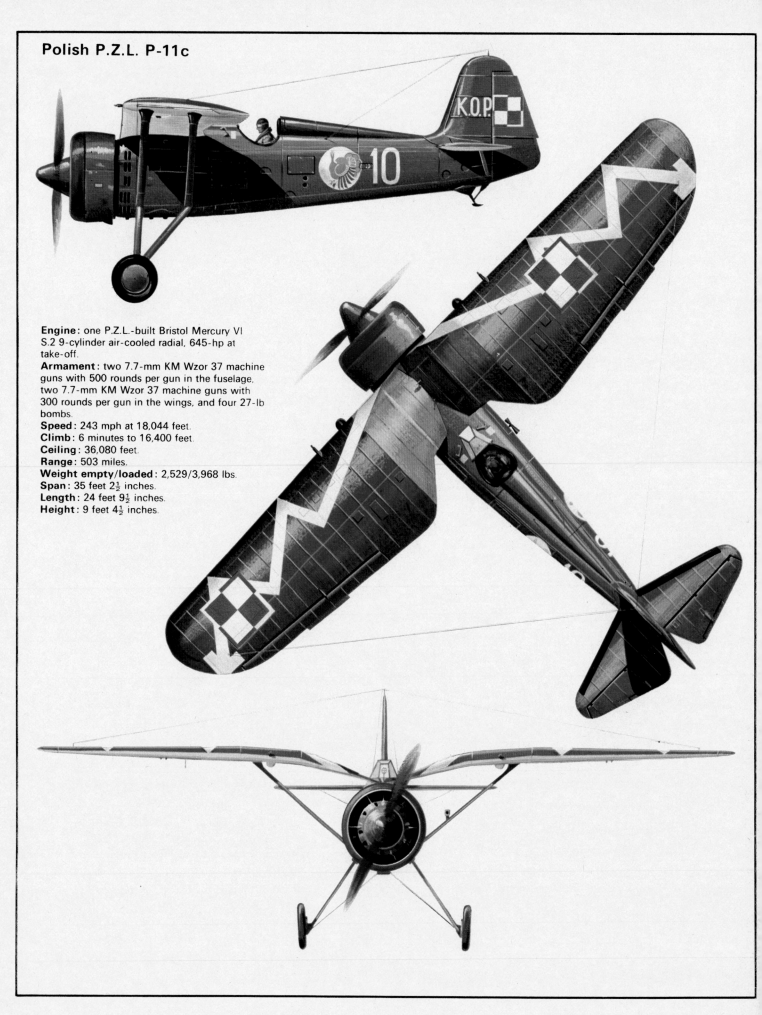

Engine: one P.Z.L.-built Bristol Mercury VI S.2 9-cylinder air-cooled radial, 645-hp at take-off.
Armament: two 7.7-mm KM Wzor 37 machine guns with 500 rounds per gun in the fuselage, two 7.7-mm KM Wzor 37 machine guns with 300 rounds per gun in the wings, and four 27-lb bombs.
Speed: 243 mph at 18,044 feet.
Climb: 6 minutes to 16,400 feet.
Ceiling: 36,080 feet.
Range: 503 miles.
Weight empty/loaded: 2,529/3,968 lbs.
Span: 35 feet 2½ inches.
Length: 24 feet 9½ inches.
Height: 9 feet 4½ inches.

German Junkers Ju 87B-1

Engine: one Junkers Jumo 211 A-1 12-cylinder
inverted-V inline, 900-hp.
Armament: two 7.9-mm MG 17 machine guns
in the wings, one 7.9-mm MG 15 in the rear
cockpit, and a maximum bomb-load of one
1,100-lb bomb on the fuselage crutch and four
110-lb bombs under the wings.
Speed: 217 mph at 16,405 feet.
Climb: 12 minutes to 13,500 feet.
Ceiling: 26,248 feet.
Range: 342 miles.
Weight empty/loaded: 6,051/9,336 lbs.
Span: 45 feet 3¼ inches.
Length: 36 feet 1 inch.
Height: 13 feet 10½ inches.
Crew: two.

CHAPTER 8
Poland's Agony

By the 17th day after France's proclamation of general mobilisation, Poland's existence as an independent state had been destroyed for the next five and a half years. There had been no precedent for such a catastrophe since Napoleon's destruction of Prussia at Jena in 1806. It was the result not so much of Poland's military weaknesses at the crucial moment as of the *matériel*, numerical, and strategic superiority of the German Army and of the Luftwaffe, helped by the fatal mistakes of the Polish High Command.

Within the frontiers which had been laid down by the Treaty of Versailles, Marshal Rydz-Smigly and his commanders had a difficult problem in planning the defence of Poland against Hitler's rearmed Germany. A glance at the map will show the reason for this. From Suwałki, on the frontier between East Prussia and Lithuania, to the Carpathians

▽ *A Heinkel He 111 unloads a stick of bombs during one of the round-the-clock air strikes of the Polish campaign.*
▷ *Vividly expressive of German air terror—"Luftwaffe", by the Polish artist B. W. Linke.*

south of Przemyśl, the Polish frontier to be defended included the Slovak border and formed a huge salient with a front line of some 1,250 miles – excluding the defence requirements of Danzig and the Corridor. To defend this vulnerable salient, the Polish High Command had only 45 divisions at its disposal.

When the Germans examined the Polish Army archives after their victory in 1939, they found that the French had given several warnings to their Polish opposite numbers about the dangers of the situation. One of them, prepared by General Weygand, the French Chief-of-Staff, had advised the Poles "to base [their] defences behind the line formed by the Rivers Niemen, Bobr, Narew, Vistula, and San". And Weygand went on to add: "From the operational point of view this concept is the only sound one, for it disposes of every possibility of envelopment and places strong river barriers in the path of German armoured formations. More important, this line is only 420 miles long, instead of the 1,250-mile front from Suwałki to the Carpathian passes."

As early as the German reoccupation of the Rhineland, Gamelin had given Rydz-Smigly the same advice during a visit to Warsaw, and he reiterated the point in his discussions with General Kasprzycki on May 16. The Polish High Command, however, replied to these French suggestions by pointing out that Poland could not continue to fight a prolonged war if she gave up the industrial regions of Upper Silesia and Łódź, and the rich agricultural regions of Kutno, Kielce, and Poznań without firing a shot. For this reason General Kutrzeba, according to the German examination of the Polish archives, proposed to include these regions in the defensive perimeter, but without stationing troops further west than the Warta river or cramming garrison forces into the Danzig Corridor, which would have meant that in the north the Polish troops were stationed where they had to face a two-front war, from German Pomerania and from East Prussia.

Whatever the reasons behind it, this was a rash plan. But when Rydz-Smigly stationed a full fifth of his resources around Poznań and in the Corridor itself

it smacked of megalomania – and he did this despite the fact that his Intelligence department had provided him with extremely accurate figures for the forces massing against Poland. Moreover, general mobilisation was not proclaimed in Poland until 1100 hours on August 31, and this meant that on the first day of the German attack the Polish front was held by only 17 infantry divisions, three infantry brigades, and six cavalry brigades. Thirteen Polish divisions mobilised by the time of the German attack were still moving to their concentration areas, while another nine divisions were still mustering in barracks.

To crown everything, the Polish High Command was fatally vulnerable in its communications with the forces in the field. There was no adequate command structure between Rydz-Smigly and his eight army commanders, and the communication network on which he depended for control in battle was cut to ribbons by the Luftwaffe's precision attacks within the first few days of the campaign.

Blitzkrieg unleashed

This unbelievable combination of mistakes contributed greatly to the Wehrmacht's success, but nothing can detract from the thoroughness of the German preparation. Brauchitsch's plan of concentration for "Case White" was based on sound concepts of strategy, and had been explained clearly to the lower command levels. Ground and air missions were co-ordinated; every man knew what he had to do; and the result got the most out of the new concept of co-operation between an armoured army and a modern air force. Drawn up at the beginning of July, the O.K.H. Directive stated: "The objective of the operation is the destruction of the Polish armed forces. The political conduct of the war demands that it be fought with crushing, surprise blows to achieve rapid success.

"Intention of the Army High Command: to disrupt, by a rapid invasion of Polish territory, the mobilisation and concentration of the Polish Army, and to destroy the bulk of troops stationed to the west of the Vistula–Narew line by converging attacks from Silesia, Pomerania, and East Prussia."

The armoured and motorised divisions

with which Germany attacked Poland totalled 55 divisions, including reserves, on "Y-Day", but by September 18 this figure had risen to 63. The front line divisions were divided into two large army groups with the following strengths and objectives:

1. **East Prussia and Pomerania** – Army Group North (Colonel-General Fedor von Bock).
   Left flank: 3rd Army (General Georg von Küchler), with eight infantry divisions, was to assist in the destruction of the Polish forces in the Corridor and drive south towards the Vistula and Warsaw.
   Right flank: 4th Army (General Günther Hans von Kluge), with six infantry divisions, two motorised divisions, and one Panzer division, was to attack from Pomerania and destroy the main body of Polish troops defending the Corridor, cutting off the Poznań-Kutno group from the north.
2. **Silesia and Slovakia** – Army Group South (Colonel-General Gerd von Rundstedt).
   Left flank: 8th Army (General Johannes Blaskowitz), with four infantry divisions and the S.S. motorised regiment *Leibstandarte Adolf Hitler*, was to engage the Polish forces in the Poznań-Kutno region and keep them from counter-attacking the central army of the group.
   Centre: 10th Army (General Walter von Reichenau), with six infantry divisions, two motorised divisions, three light divisions, and two Panzer divisions, was to drive north-east, straight for Wieluń, Łódź, and Warsaw.
   Right flank: 14th Army (General Sigmund Wilhelm List), with one mountain division, six infantry divisions, one light division, two Panzer divisions, and the S.S. motorised regiment *Germania*, was to strike across the Carpathians from Slovakia and pin down the Polish forces around Kraków and Przemyśl.

Hitler, however, intervened and altered Army Group North's schedule. By switching its forces east of Warsaw, he made sure that any Polish forces which managed to cross the Vistula would be cut off to the east of the Capital.

For General Guderian, however, the opening of the German offensive started with near disaster. He was in command of XIX Panzer Corps and, a sound armour tactician, was well up with his forward

△ *German troops advance into Danzig, which after so many months of impassioned propaganda was a mere backwater of the main campaign.*
▷ *Balance of forces for the campaign. The Wehrmacht's advantages were increased by the Polish attempt to defend their territory west of the Vistula – a fatally weak deployment.*
▷▷ *One of the rare pauses during the German thrust towards Warsaw.*

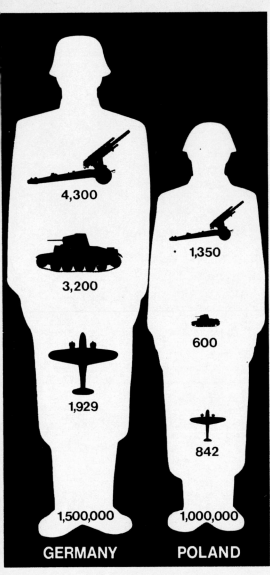

GERMANY	POLAND
4,300	1,350
3,200	600
1,929	842
1,500,000	1,000,000

WARSZAWA 347
NOWA KARCZMA 14
KOŚCIERZYNA 22
ŻUKOWO 16

117605

The Polish Campaign

0   100   200 km

POLWYSEP HEL

MEMEL

LITHUANIA

POLOTZK

KONIGSBERG   KAUNAS   VILNA

GDYNIA
DANZIG

GERMANY
3rd Army

MINSK

Army Group North
(or "B")
4th Army

TCZEW

SUWALKI

STETTIN

PO

CHELMNO

TORUN

M

BIALYSTOK

Narew

U.

MODLIN

N

W

Niemen

Oder

FRANKFURT

PN

POZNAN   GNIEZNO

KUTNO

WARSAW

Bug

S.

BREST-LITOVSK

GLOGAU

WARTA

Bzura

LODZ

GORA KALWARIA
DEBLIN

S.

8th Army

WIELUN

PR

PIOTRKOW

PY

BRESLAU

L

10th Army

CZESTOCHOWA

P O L A N D

G

OPPELN

SANDOMIERZ

TOMASZOW

Army Group South
(or "A")

K

San

L'VOV

R.

E

OSTRAVA

KRAKOW

CA PRZEMYSL

Dniestr

R

JABLONIKA

DUKLA

M

14th Army

LUPKOW

A

USZOK

N

SLOVAKIA
BRATISLAVA

Y

HUNGARY

RUMANIA

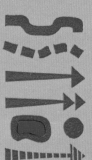

: German armies.

: Frontier defence units.

: German attacks (September 1–9).

: German attacks (September 10–17).

: Polish pockets.

: Soviet invasion (September 17).

: Frontiers on September 1

N : Polish armies.

: Partition line agreed by the Treaty of Delimitation (September 28).

N : Narew (Mlot-Fijalkowski), 18th & 33rd Infantry Divisions, "Suwałki" & "Podlaska" Cavalry Brigades.

M : Modlin (Przedrzymirski), 8th & 20th Infantry Divisions, "Mazow & "Nowogrod" Cavalry Brigades.

PO : Pomeranian (Bortnowski), 4th, 9th, 15th, 16th, & 27th Infantry Divisions, "Pomerania" Cavalry Brigade.

PN : Poznań (Kutrzeba), 14th, 17th, 25th, & 26th Infantry Divisions, "Great Poland" & "Podolia" Cavalry Brigades.

L : Łódź (Rommel), 2nd, 10th, 28th, & 30th Infantry Divisions, "Border" & "Wolhynia" Cavalry Brigades.

K : Kraków (Szylling), 6th, 7th, 21st, 23rd, 45th, & 55th Infantry Divisions, "Kraków" Cavalry Brigade.

CA : Carpathian (Fabryci), 11th, 24th, & 38th Infantry Divisions, 2nd & 3rd Mountain Brigades.

PR : Prussian (Dab-Biernacki), 3rd, 12th, 13th, 19th, 29th, & 36th Infantry Divisions, "Vilna" Cavalry Brigade.

PY : Pyskór Group, 39th Infantry Division & "Warsaw" Armoured Brigade.

W : Wyskow Group (Skwarczinski), 1st, 35th & 41st Infantry Divisions. In addition, the 5th & 44th Infantry Divisions were moving up to Kutno, and the 22nd & 38th to Przemyśl.

troops. "The corps crossed the frontier simultaneously at 0445 hours on September 1," he later recalled. "There was a thick ground mist at first which prevented the Luftwaffe from giving us any support. I drove forward with the 3rd Panzer Brigade in the first wave [until it came into action]. Contrary to my orders, the 3rd Panzer Brigade's heavy artillery felt itself compelled to fire into the mist. The first shell landed 50 yards in front of my command vehicle, the second 50 yards behind. I was sure that the next one would be a direct hit and ordered my driver to turn about and drive off. The unaccustomed noise had made him nervous, however, and he drove flat-out straight into a ditch. The front axle of the half-track was bent so that the steering mechanism was put out of action. This marked the end of my drive . . ."

The Blitzkrieg triumphant

The first stage of the campaign saw the Polish cavalry of the "Pomorze Army" (Pomeranian Army), under General Bortnowski, charge the tanks of Guderian's XIX Panzer Corps as they thrust across the Corridor towards the Vistula, which they crossed at Chełmno on September 6, making contact with 3rd Army on the far bank. As late as September 15–18, when the campaign was already lost, the Polish "Sosnkowski Group" (11th and 38th Divisions), marching by night and fighting by day, managed three times to break through the ring which the German 14th Army was trying to close behind it. Fighting their way across the San river, the Sosnkowski divisions managed to capture 20 guns and 180 vehicles from 14th Army.

All this was achieved under non-stop bombing raids by the Luftwaffe. Although the Polish Air Force managed to keep up sporadic air attack up to September 17, the Luftwaffe dominated the air. *Luftflotten* (Air Fleets) I and IV, commanded by Generals Albert Kesselring and Alexander Löhr, concentrated their attacks on communication centres, pockets of resistance, and Polish forces on the move. *Luftflotte* I operated with Bock's Army Group North, *Luftflotte* IV with Rundstedt's Army Group South. Between them, the two air fleets totalled 897 bombers and 219 Stukas.

The advantage of unchallenged air power helped the German 10th Army to win rapid successes in its advance on

△ *In the path of the Stukas: a smashed Polish supply column. Both sides relied heavily upon horse-drawn supply vehicles – but only the Germans had Stukas.*
◁ *Dejected in defeat: Polish cavalrymen, their faces drawn with fatigue, continue their retreat before the remorseless advance of the Panzer divisions.*

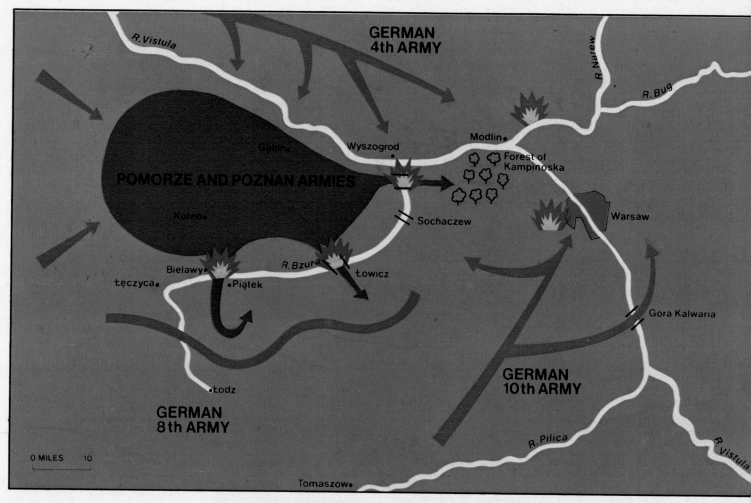

GERMAN
4th ARMY

R. Vistula

R. Narew

R. Bug

POMORZE AND POZNAN ARMIES

Gąbin

Wyszogrod

Modlin

Forest of Kampinoska

Kutno

Sochaczew

Warsaw

Bielawy

R. Bzura

Łowicz

Łęczyca

Piątek

Gora Kalwaria

Łodz

GERMAN
10th ARMY

GERMAN
8th ARMY

R. Pilica

R. Vistula

0 MILES 10

Tomaszow

△ The Battle of the Bzura, when the scales nearly tilted. The ponderous Polish thrusts across the Bzura caught the German forces advancing upon Warsaw in flank – but Rundstedt's hastily-formed front south-east of the river, and accurate Stuka strikes at the Bzura bridges, converted the dangerous counter-attack into a battle of encirclement.

▷ German artillery bombarding Warsaw, by the German artist Franz Eichhorst. The gallant but fruitless resistance of the Polish capital was maintained until the 28th – a murderous siege of 14 days.

Warsaw. It is true that on September 8 its 4th Panzer Division failed in its attempt to take Warsaw by surprise, but two days later 10th Army reached the Vistula at Góra Kalwaria and tore the Polish "Łódź Army" to shreds. At the same time the Polish "Prussian Army" had also been cut off, broken up, and destroyed in a battle against heavy odds. Marshal Rydz-Śmigly's order for the Polish armies to withdraw eastwards had gone out on September 6, but it was already too late.

This withdrawal led to one of the most dramatic episodes in the Polish campaign. Falling back on Warsaw, the "Pomorze" and "Poznań" Armies were challenged by the German 8th Army, coming up from Łódz, which tried to bar their retreat. The result was the hard-fought "Battle of the Bzura", which began on September 10. The Polish troops succeeded in capturing bridgeheads across the Bzura river near Łowicz, and drove back the German 30th Infantry Division. Thanks to Hitler's order to switch the advance east of Warsaw, Army Group North was unable to intervene fast enough to cover the flank of Army Group South. But Rundstedt rose to the crisis. While Stukas attacked the

Bzura bridgeheads, the motorised and Panzer divisions of 10th Army wheeled north and caught the Polish forces in flank. There was vicious fighting around Łowicz and Sochaczew before the Poles pulled back; but at last, completely cut off and hemmed in about Kutno, General Bortnowski was forced to order the surrender of his 170,000 men on September 19.

While 8th Army closed the inner pincers of the German advance by investing Warsaw and Modlin, the plan imposed by Hitler aimed at a wider sweep to trap the remaining Polish fragments retreating east of the Vistula. This was achieved by a deep Panzer penetration led by Guderian. His XIX Panzer Corps had been transferred across East Prussia after its initial successes in the Corridor, and on September 9 it forced the Narew river upstream of Łomza. Six days later it had driven as far south as Brest Litovsk, and its 3rd Panzer Division, pressing south towards Włodawa, had made contact with advance units of 10th and 14th Armies from Army Group South. 14th Army, which had advanced eastwards as far as L'vov, had swung north-east to complete this link-up.

△ German troops in the ruins of Warsaw. ▽ Tribute to Luftwaffe accuracy: a neatly-bombed bridge. Pinpoint attacks against the communications formed one of the most effective elements in the pattern of the Blitzkrieg.

Stab in the back from Stalin

Until this moment the Soviet Union had observed the letter of the Soviet–Polish Non-Aggression Pact of 1932, which, renewed on May 5, 1934, was intended to run until the end of 1945. But when it became obvious that the destruction of the Polish Army was imminent, Moscow decided to intervene in order to make sure of the territories (east of the line formed by the Narew, Vistula, and San rivers) conceded to the Soviet Union by the secret protocol attached to the German–Soviet Non-Aggression Pact. At 0300 hours on September 17, Vladimir Potemkin, Deputy Commissar for Foreign Affairs, told Polish Ambassador Grzybowski that "the fact is that the Polish State and its Government have ceased to exist".

"For this reason," ran the note which Potemkin read to Grzybowski, "the treaties concluded between the Soviet Union and Poland have lost their validity. Abandoned to its own fate and deprived of its rulers, Poland has become an area in which could develop all manner of circumstances potentially dangerous to the Soviet Union. This is why, having maintained its neutrality up to now, the Soviet Union cannot remain neutral in the present situation.

"The Soviet Union can no longer remain indifferent to the sufferings of its blood-brothers the Ukrainians and Belorussians, who, inhabitants of Polish territory, are being abandoned to their fate and left defenceless. In consideration of this situation the Soviet Government has ordered the High Command of the Red Army to send its troops across the frontier and to take under their protection the lives and welfare of the populations of the western Ukraine and western Belorussia." The note had been drawn up with the full agreement of Germany, which had undertaken not to conclude an armistice with Poland.

The Polish Ambassador refused to accept this note, but a few hours later large Red Army forces crossed the frontier and pushed motorised and armoured columns westward towards Vilna, Brest-Litovsk, Kovel', and L'vov. Within days their spearheads had made contact with Wehrmacht troops in Galicia and along the River Bug.

The intervention of the Red Army ended the last vain hopes of the Polish High Command for prolonging resistance in a last-ditch campaign in eastern Galicia with their backs to the Rumanian frontier. On the morning of September 18, President Mościcki, Colonel Beck, and the remainder of the Polish Government, together with Marshal Rydz-Smigly, fled to Rumania and claimed political asylum. Poland's formal resistance was over.

Poland: erased from the map of Europe

During this 18-day campaign the German armies had largely over-run the demarcation line agreed between Stalin and

▽ It was their battle, too: apprehensive Warsaw citizens scan the sky to detect the next wave of Luftwaffe bombers.
▷ Polish prisoners of war. Their war was over – but thousands of their compatriots escaped to the West through Rumania and carried on the fight from France and Britain.

Ribbentrop on August 23. This led to a new settlement between Moscow and Berlin: the "German-Soviet Treaty of Delimitation and Friendship", signed on September 28 by Ribbentrop after another journey to Moscow. The agreement, which split Poland in two, was made at Stalin's insistence, as he refused to countenance a German suggestion for the establishment of a Polish state of 15 million inhabitants.

In this partition agreement, Germany accepted the inclusion of Lithuania into the Soviet sphere of influence; in compensation, the parts of the province of Warsaw already conceded in the agreement of August 23, plus the entire province of Lublin, were conceded to Germany. In central Poland the new demarcation line connected the Vistula and Bug rivers; in Galicia it remained on the San river, for Stalin refused to give up the petroleum wells of Drohobycz and Boryslaw.

Another protocol declared that the Soviet Union would not make any difficulties for citizens of Estonia, Latvia, and Lithuania who might wish to leave the Soviet zone of influence, taking their

personal goods with them. In this agreement, Stalin and Hitler renewed the anti-Polish engagements which had bound together the Romanovs and Hohenzollerns in Imperial days. "The undersigned plenipotentiaries, on concluding the German-Soviet Treaty of Delimitation and Friendship, have declared their agreement on the following points:

"The two parties will tolerate in their territories no Polish agitation affecting the territory of the other party. They will suppress in their territories all beginnings of such agitation and inform each other concerning suitable measures for this purpose."

The same day, September 28, Warsaw surrendered after 14 days of heroic resistance. Luftwaffe bombing had set the city flourmills ablaze, and the filtration and pumping stations for the water supply had been more than half destroyed. A humane commander, General Blaskowitz of the German 8th Army allowed the honours of war to Warsaw's defenders, who had been galvanised by their leader, General Rommel, formerly the commander of the "Łódź

Heinz Guderian, architect of the Panzer force. His pre-war ideas on the correct use of armour had won Hitler's approval, and his leadership in the Polish campaign had completely vindicated them. After sweeping through the Danzig Corridor, his Panzer corps was switched to the eastern flank and formed the northern jaws of the pincers which trapped the Polish armies at Brest Litovsk.

Army". Among the prisoners-of-war was General Kutrzeba, who had broken out of the Kutno pocket with four divisions. Modlin capitulated a few hours before Warsaw.

The last shots of the campaign were fired in the Półwysep Hel peninsula, north of Danzig, where Admiral Unruh surrendered with 4,500 men on October 2.

When Hitler broadcast to the German people on September 30, he announced the number of Polish prisoners taken as 694,000, compared with German losses of 10,572 killed, 3,400 missing, presumed dead, and 30,322 wounded. These figures support Guderian's comment to Hitler on September 5, when the latter visited Guderian's sector: "Tanks are a life-saving weapon."

From the time of the first successes won by the German Army in Poland, Hitler had made constant visits to the front-line areas to judge the importance of the victories for himself. "On October 5," General von Manstein recalled, "a big military parade was held, which unfortunately ended with a disagreeable incident showing Hitler's bizarre attitude towards his generals. We were accompanying him on his return to the airfield, and we felt that at least we might expect a few words of thanks. A table had been laid at which Hitler and his generals could sample some soup prepared by the field kitchens. But when he saw the white tablecloth and the flower decorations which had been provided in his honour, Hitler turned brusquely aside, tasted two or three mouthfuls of soup, chatted briefly with the soldiers, and got straight into his aeroplane. Apparently he

△ *October 5, 1939: Adolf Hitler reviews his victorious troops in Warsaw. "He made a speech to his soldiers," recalled American journalist William Shirer; "the speech of a conquering Caesar."*

wanted to show his close ties with the people. But I doubt that this gesture was really to the taste of our brave grenadiers, who would have understood perfectly that if the Head of State chose to eat with his generals he would be paying equal homage to the troops. For us, it was an affront which gave us much food for thought."

For its part, the Red Army rounded up some 217,000 prisoners, many of whom were destined to die in Russia in circumstances that will be examined in due course. About 100,000 Poles managed to escape to the West via Rumania and carry on the fight against Germany from France and Britain.

All quiet on the Western Front...

On September 13, General Georges, commanding the French North-East Front,

taking Poland's defeat as virtually completed, ordered General Prételat "not to advance beyond the objectives attained but to strengthen your dispositions in depth and to arrange as soon as possible for replacement divisions to relieve your front-line divisions, in particular the motorised divisions".

So ended Operation "Saar", which had cost the French Army 27 killed, 2? wounded, and 28 missing. General Vuille min's air force had lost nine fighters and 18 reconnaissance aircraft. Both Gamelir and Georges later justified this decision to halt operations against Germany on the following grounds. Everything suggested that with Poland annihilated, Hitler would turn against the West with his full strength, with the assurance of a superiority of about 100 divisions to 60. More over, it was possible that Mussolini drawn by the ease with which Poland had been conquered, might attack France himself before the Alpine passes were snowed up and rendered impassable.

CHAPTER 9
Western Front: the rival plans

On September 27, after his return to Berlin, Hitler summoned Generals von Brauchitsch and Halder and told them why, in his opinion, an immediate offensive should be launched in the West.

In his diary, Halder recorded the basic points of Hitler's arguments: "The Führer will try to use the impression created by our victory in Poland to come to an arrangement.

"Should this fail, the fact that time is working for the enemy rather than for us means that we will have to strike in the West, and do so as soon as possible.

. Belgium's apparent renunciation of her neutrality threatens the Ruhr Valley. This means that we must gain sufficient territory to serve as a wide protective area for our interests.

. The advantage given us by the enemy's present weakness in anti-tank and anti-aircraft guns will diminish with time. This means that our superiority in tanks and aircraft will progressively disappear.

. Britain's war effort is only getting under way now, and it will increase. This makes it necessary to plan an offensive in the West between October 20 and 25. Striking across Holland and Belgium, this would:

(a) Gain the Belgian-Dutch coast, which would give us a base for an air offensive against England;

(b) Crush the Allied military forces in the field; and

(c) Gain for ourselves in northern France sufficient territory to extend the system of our air and naval bases."

The "arrangement" proposed to the Western powers by Hitler in his speech to the Reichstag on October 5 was rejected by both France and Great Britain. Neither power was going to accept Hitler's suggestion and accept tamely the partition of Poland, which had been settled by the treaty signed in Moscow on September 28. On October 9, therefore, in his Directive No. 6, Hitler defined the missions which must be undertaken by the Army, the Navy, and the Luftwaffe in this offensive. This decision came as a surprise to the O.K.H., which had not studied any such project for 20 years. But Hitler over-ruled the objections of Halder and Brauchitsch with a direct order, and on October 19 they

▽ "Britain! This is your work!" The poster is German propaganda from September 1939, but the anguished condemnation could have been raised with some considerable justification by conquered Poland. For Britain and France were treaty-bound to aid Poland; in the short course of the Polish campaign Britain had given no help, and France had launched only a token offensive that had disturbed the German plans not one jot. The Allies had gone to war convinced of Poland's ability to hold out, but even so, there were no plans for giving Poland any direct aid.

ANGLIO! TWOJE DZIEŁO!

Bock

Rundstedt

Leeb

Küchler

Reichenau

Manstein

Kluge

Weichs

List

Busch

The German line up that defeated France. Although there was great dissension and rivalry as to which army group was to deliver the main blow, once Hitler had given his orders there was to be no more prevarication. O.K.H. had originally assigned the major rôle to Army Group "B" in the north, but the Chief-of-Staff of Army Group "A", Manstein, and his commander, Rundstedt, thought this wrong. They felt that the "right hook", as used in World War I, was not capable of producing decisive results. Manstein was of the opinion that Army Group "A" should be made the main striking force, and that the German offensive should be a "left hook" through Sedan and up to the Channel coast.

presented a preliminary plan of operations entitled *"Fall Gelb"* ("Case Yellow") which was revised in detail and produced again on the 29th.

"Case Yellow"–the revised German plan

Using a total of 102 divisions, of which nine were armoured and six motorised, the plan entrusted the offensive to a strong right wing, which was to destroy the Allied forces north of the Somme and gain possession of Dunkirk and Boulogne. With this aim in mind, Bock's Army Group "B" was especially reinforced to 43 divisions and was to attack west of Luxembourg on both sides of Liège.

Bock's right-wing army (6th Army–Reichenau) contained five Panzer divisions; its objective was Ghent. On the left, Kluge's 4th Army would drive on Thuin on the Sambre (nine miles south-west of Charleroi) with four Panzer divisions. This armoured wedge would be covered on the north flank (Antwerp) by Küchler's 18th Army and on the south flank (Givet) by General von Weichs' 2nd Army.

Meanwhile, Rundstedt's Army Group "A" would attack further to the south with 12th Army (List) and 16th Army (General Ernst Busch) on a front connecting Laon, Carignan, and Longwy. Rundstedt's army group had only 22 divisions, all of them infantry. Facing the Maginot Line, from Thionville south along the Rhine to Basle, Leeb's Army Group "C" (1st and 7th Armies) would remain on the defensive with its 18 divisions.

Held in general reserve, under the orders of O.K.H., were 19 divisions, of which two were motorised.

According to the plan of October 29, the neutral territory of Holland would only be violated in the "appendix" of territory around Maastricht, which would be crossed by 6th Army in its westward drive. Queen Wilhelmina's Government would be left to decide whether or not this constituted a *casus belli*. But Göring feared that the Dutch Government would react to this cavalier treatment by allowing the R.A.F. to use air bases in Holland for a bomber offensive, and for this reason it was decided to extend the offensive to include the invasion of Holland.

At the time, Hitler raised no objection to the plan put before him by O.K.H.; but in Koblenz Lieutenant-General Erich von

Manstein, Chief-of-Staff of Army Group "A", regarded the plan with little enthusiasm. On October 31 he wrote: "It is conceivable that we will meet with the initial success hoped for against Belgium and the forces which the Allies will rush to her aid. But initial success does not mean total victory. This can only come from the *complete destruction* of all enemy forces in the field, both in Belgium and north of the Somme. At the same time we must be able to cope with the French counter-offensive which is certain to come from the south or the south-west."

In this first memorandum, which Rundstedt endorsed and forwarded to O.K.H. under his signature, Manstein's criticisms were complemented by a suggestion. These considerations argue that the *centre of gravity [Schwerpunkt] of the entire operation* should be transferred to Army Group 'A''s southern flank . . . "Operating south of Liège, it should drive across the Meuse upstream of Namur and push westwards along the Arras-Boulogne axis, in such a way as to cut off along the Somme all the forces which the enemy dares to push forward into Belgium, and not only throw him back to the Somme."

Did Halder and Brauchitsch interpret these suggestions as a desire on Rundstedt's part to obtain a more prestigious role for himself in *Fall Gelb*? Whatever the reasons, Manstein's suggestions were not passed on from O.K.H. to O.K.W. *Oberkommando der Wehrmacht*, or the High Command of the German Armed Forces). Nor were Manstein's memoranda of November 21, November 30, December , and December 18, in which he further improved and expanded his basic idea.

Hitler changes the plan

Hitler, therefore, was unaware of Manstein's plan when, on November 9, he announced that he considered the armour in the southern wing to be too weak, and on the 15th ordered the transfer to Army Group "A" of Guderian's XIX Panzer Corps—two Panzer divisions, one motorised division, the motorised regiment *Grossdeutschland*, and the S.S. Regiment *Leibstandarte Adolf Hitler*. Guderian's Corps was to drive across the wooded terrain of the Ardennes through Arlon, Mantigny, and Florenville and "secure a bridgehead across the Meuse at Sedan which will create favourable conditions

FRENCH ARMY and B.E.F.

Gamelin

Georges

Billotte

Giraud

Gort

Huntziger

Corap

Blanchard

The Allied High Command. This was overly complex, with inadequately defined chain of command structures. The result was to prove disastrous: the Allied commanders failed to work together to produce a plan that had any chance of halting the Germans.

for the pursuit of operations if the armoured units of 6th and 4th Armies should fail to break through".

On the 20th, Hitler went even further towards falling in with the Manstein plan when he ordered O.K.H. to make preparations for transferring the main weight of the coming offensive from Bock's army group to that of Rundstedt, "in case the actual enemy dispositions, as they appear now, turn out to offer greater and more rapid successes to [Army Group 'A']". This was no hypothesis. In October, the cryptology team on the general staff of Army Group "C", helped by the top experts from O.K.H., had broken the radio code used by the French High Command. This striking success was not revealed to the public until 1959 by General Liss, the former head of O.K.H. Military Intelligence (Section West), and it means that several former judgements on the campaign of May-June 1940 have had to be revised. Liss claims that "the bulk of the radio traffic between the French War Ministry in the Rue St. Dominique with the army groups, the armies, and the authorities of the Interior, North Africa, and Syria, gradually came into our hands. The change of code which was made every four weeks held us

"nous vaincrons parceque nous sommes les plus forts"

SOUSCRIVEZ AUX BONS d'ARMEMENT

up for only a few days."

So it was that the Germans listened in to many secrets of the organisation and armament of their enemies and learned much of inestimable value. While preparing a major offensive based on the use of armour, they were able, for example, to learn that the general supply of the French 25-mm anti-tank gun was being badly delayed. It was extremely foolish of the French to transmit, and thereby leak, so many secrets of this nature over the air.

Belgium: the Allied plan

In the Allied camp, the French *Deuxième Bureau* (Secret Service) had been following the German build-up on the frontiers of Holland and Belgium right from the start, and it had arrived at an estimated figure which was very close to the actual total of German divisions in the West. The *Deuxième Bureau's* opinion was that the Germans would attack as soon as possible with about 100 divisions, of which ten would be armoured, and that they would launch their main offensive across the open terrain of Holland.

Given this Intelligence, the French and the British had a difficult choice.

On the one hand, the Allies could stand fast on their position along the frontier. This is basically what the new Prime Minister, Paul Reynaud, put to the French War Ministry on April 9, 1940. In his memoirs he says: "So it was that having

said in the years before war 'If you want t[o] go into Belgium, arm yourselves', I sai[d] on April 9, 1940: 'Unless you are armed, d[o] not go into Belgium.' "

Gamelin later denied that Reynaud sai[d] any such thing – a controversy that will b[e] examined in due course. But the fac[t] remains that in September 1939 neithe[r] the French nor the British felt that the[y] could adopt so supine a strategy. And thi[s] opened the way for the second alternative[:] an advance across the border into Belgium[.]

The solemn guarantee made to the[ ] nation of Belgium by the two Allie[d] governments meant that they were dut[y] bound to come to Belgium's aid and t[o] help her beat off an invasion. But there[ ] were other considerations apart from[ ] honour.

1. For Great Britain, it was vital that the[ ] Belgian coast should be denied to the[ ] Germans, for she had bitter memorie[s] of the damage done by Belgian-base[d] U-boats between 1915 and 1918. It wa[s] also clear that Belgium's potential a[s] an advance base for the Luftwaffe wa[s] too great to be tolerated.

2. France felt that trench warfare along[ ] her northern frontier would endange[r] the industrial region behind it. Any[ ] stoppage of work in the steelworks o[f] Denain, Valenciennes, or Fives-Lill[e] would have disastrous results on the[ ] output of armoured vehicles.

3. By the time the first two corps of the[ ] British Expeditionary Force (B.E.F.) had entered the line at Lille on Octobe[r] 12, General Georges still had only 72

Allied divisions to pit against 102 German. If he could add the 30-odd Belgian and Dutch divisions to his strength, he could meet any German offensive on equal terms. If Georges left the Belgians and Dutch to face defeat or capitulation, he would have to hold the French frontier with a force of seven against ten.

The Escaut manoeuvre

This was why General André Laffargue spoke out against Reynaud's arguments in his book *Justice for the Men of 1940:* "Under these conditions, the 'Frontier' solution demanded 36 divisions, of which we had only 32. It also implied that we would not have the benefit of the Belgian and Dutch divisions, which over-strained our dispositions and put our line into a state of 'pre-rupture'." By May 10, 1940, many more reinforcements had joined the Allied front, but in October 1939, General Gaston Henri Billotte, commanding the 1st Army Group, had considerably weaker forces at his disposal.

Italy's non-belligerence and the freezing-up of the Alpine passes had enabled Billotte and his general staff to be moved north from their original base at Lyons. General Georges put Billotte in command of the sector of the front between Longuyon and the North Sea, and on October 24 gave him provisional orders "if the C.-in-C. Land Forces (Gamelin) should decide to move into Belgium in order to accept battle on the Escaut".

If this decision were made, the French 2nd, 9th, and 1st Armies, commanded respectively by Generals Charles Huntziger, André Corap, and Georges Blanchard, would remain in position along the French frontier between Longuyon and Maulde-sur-Escaut. Only the B.E.F. (General Lord Gort) and the French XVI Corps (General Fagalde) were to move eastwards into Belgium. The former was to take up position around Tournai, and the latter was to move further downstream on the Escaut, establish a bridgehead at Ghent, and make contact with the Belgian forces as they fell back from the Albert Canal. The day after the alert of November 9, the French 7th Army (General Henri Giraud), in reserve around Rheims, was ordered to join the XVI Corps.

The weakness of the Escaut Line was that it over-stretched the front to be defended, and that the Allied forces on the Escaut would hardly be assisted by the remnants of the Belgian Army falling back from the line of the Albert Canal with the German tanks on their heels. For this reason, the "personal and secret instruction" of October 24 envisaged a much deeper Allied advance into Belgium. General Billotte was ordered to keep his forces in readiness "for the right circumstances and the order of the general commanding the North-East Theatre of Operations, and then, while remaining in position on French soil between Rochonvilliers and Revin, to advance in force to the line Louvain-Wavre-Gembloux-Namur. To the south the front will be secure by the occupation of the Meuse between Givet and Namur; in the north the British forces on the Dyle will be in touch on their left with the Belgian forces defending Antwerp."

This "Dyle Plan", as it became known, gave the Allies a much shorter front to defend and meant that the Belgians would not have to retreat far before joining the relieving armies. The plan required King Léopold III and the Belgian High Command to keep their allies fully informed of their strategic intentions in the event of German aggression. The alert of November 9 led to the first exchange of information between the Belgian and French supreme headquarters, and on the 14th General Georges converted the provisional Dyle Plan into a definite order.

As soon as the Belgian Goverment appealed to the French, the 9th Army would advance to a line Mezières–Namur with its units deployed west of the Meuse; 1st Army would take up position between Namur and Wavre; and the B.E.F. would hold the line between Wavre and Louvain, where it would establish contact with the Belgian Army. Giraud's 7th Army would be held in reserve west of Antwerp.

The steady rain of late autumn 1939 forced Hitler at the last moment to call off the offensive which he had ordered for November 12. Between then and January 16, 1940, the elements intervened no less than 13 times to postpone *Fall Gelb* – much to the relief of the German generals, who had the gloomiest view of the plan. They remembered the tenacity of the French at Verdun in 1916, against whom many of the German General Staff had fought as captains or majors. But the former corporal of World War I had other ideas, which led to several appalling scenes with Brauchitsch.

△ *A jibe intended to shake the morale of thousands of unwilling reservists in France: "Forward, sons of France! . . . for England".*

△ *Fair comment on divided aims and command. Daladier asks Chamberlain: "When shall we start?" "Start what?" "The war!" "What war?"*

▽ *"No, my old friend, nothing's changed since 1914 . . . It's still the same old Germany." Though not true politically, it was in practical military terms: the German Army crashed through France's frontier defences in 1940 as it had in 1914.*

CHAPTER 10
THE SEA WAR:
Scapa Flow and the Plate

Hitler approached the war at sea with caution. On September 3 the German U-boats were ordered to confine their operations strictly to the limits laid down by the London Convention of 1936 in their attacks against British merchant shipping, and were not to attack passenger liners or French shipping. Hitler did not want to launch an all-out effort against the Western Allies at sea – but above all he wanted to avoid incidents like the sinking of the *Lusitania* in May 1915, which had helped bring the United States into World War I.

"The Battle of the River Plate" by Norman Wilkinson. In the centre of the painting is the Achilles, *firing at the* Graf Spee *(on the horizon). Behind the New Zealand light cruiser can be seen her sister ship* Ajax.

On September 24 the restrictions on attacking French shipping were lifted, and on the 27th a free hand was also given to the pocket-battleships *Graf Spee* and *Deutschland*, which had sailed for their "waiting areas" in the North Atlantic several days before the opening of hostilities.

This first phase of the war at sea – September–December 1939 – closed with the Allies slightly on top. The U-boats had scored a total of 114 Allied and neutral merchantmen sunk, with an aggregate tonnage of 421,156. Most of these ships, however, had been isolated sailings, as France and Great Britain had decided to reintroduce the highly successful convoy system which had beaten the

U-boats in World War I. By the end of the year, only four ships sailing in convoys had been lost to U-boats. Another fact which favoured the Allies was that the magnetic pistols which detonated the German torpedoes were grossly inefficient and remained so for months. When they did not detonate prematurely – which happened on September 17, saving the British aircraft-carrier *Ark Royal* – they often failed to detonate at all on reaching the target.

Hence the typically disgusted message from Lieutenant-Commander Zahn of *U-56* on October 30. "1000 hours: *Rodney*, *Nelson*, *Hood* [two battleships and a battle-cruiser in company – a submariner's dream target] and ten destroyers in Square 3492, steering 240. Three torpedoes launched. Detonators failed." The U-boat crew had heard the clang of three hits on *Nelson*'s hull. (Despite the claim made by Dönitz in his memoirs, First Lord of the Admiralty Winston Churchill was not on board.)

The Royal Navy's struggle against the U-boats was greatly assisted by the "Asdic" equipment. This was developed at the end of World War I by a committee of Allied scientists; hence the name "Asdic" – Allied Submarine Detection Investigation Committee (the device was known to the U.S. Navy as "Sonar"). Asdic was an ultra-sonic detector which could pick up echoes (from impulses sent out by the apparatus) reflected by submarines – but it needed skilful use, and in the opening months of the war it did not achieve the miracles expected of it. Nevertheless, by December 31, 1939, nine U-boats had been sunk. Six of these were ocean going, and the German U-boat arm had had only 25 ocean-going U-boats at the outbreak of war.

Battle of the River Plate

The pocket-battleships, despite the enormous range given them by their diesel engines, also failed to live up to their expectations. *Deutschland* had left Wilhelmshaven on August 24 for her first North Atlantic war cruise. By the time she was recalled to German waters on November 1, she had sunk only two merchantmen of 7,000 gross tons. On her arrival at her new base, the former Polish port of Gdynia (which Hitler had renamed Gotenhafen), *Deutschland* was rechrist

▽ Graf Spee *in happier days. A view forward from the starboard side of the ship before the war. The structure in the foreground is part of the rangefinder for the secondary director control equipment, which played so important a part in holding off the British light cruisers at the Plate.*

	Aircraft Carriers	Battleships, Battle-Cruisers and Pocket Battleships	Cruisers	Destroyers	Escort Vessels	Submarines	Totals
GREAT BRITAIN	11	17	76	243	52	51	450
FRANCE	2	9	19	76	42	78	226
GERMANY	1	9	11	41	11	57	130

△ *The naval balance of forces at the opening of hostilities, in ships built or launched. Note that even in submarines the German Navy was outnumbered by the French alone.*

▽ *The cruise of the* Graf Spee (left), *the Battle of the River Plate* (below), *and the pursuit to Montevideo* (bottom), *with the crippled* Exeter *limping away for a refit in the Falklands.*

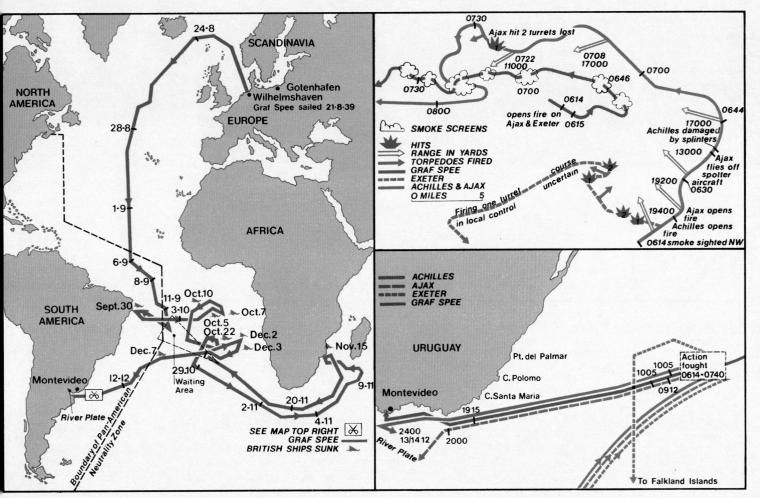

121

▷ ▽ *Captain Hans Langsdorff with members of his crew. Distressed by his casualties in the action off the Plate and despairing of chances of breaking through to Germany, Langsdorff ordered the scuttling of his ship in Montevideo Roads and later committed suicide.* ▷ *"Main object of the attack: the aircraft carrier"–a page from the* Völkischer Beobachter *of October 11, 1939, claiming that a German pilot had sunk the British* Ark Royal *on September 26. In fact the pilot, Lieutenant Adolf Francke, had dropped his bomb off the Ark Royal's bow, and had not claimed the sinking of the ship. But the Propaganda Ministry had seized the story and convinced the German people of the* Ark Royal's *loss. Francke was awarded the Iron Cross, but he became the object of so much ridicule within the Luftwaffe that he was nearly driven to suicide.*

ened, in deference to Hitler's obsession that no warship named after the Fatherland should be risked at sea. So *Deutschland* became *Lützow*, the former German heavy cruiser of that name having been handed over to the Soviet Union.

In the South Atlantic, the *Graf Spee* was off Pernambuco (Brazil) when on September 27 her commander, Captain Hans Langsdorff, received the order to commence operations against Allied merchant shipping. *Graf Spee*'s war cruise lasted 77 days, taking her at one time eastwards into the Indian Ocean and sending to the bottom nine merchantmen totalling 50,000 tons. Dawn on December 13 found *Graf Spee* heading for the shipping focus of the River Plate area for a last foray before returning to Germany. Instead, *Graf Spee*'s lookouts sighted Commodore H. H. Harwood's South Atlantic cruiser squadron, which immediately prepared to give battle.

„Schwerpunkt des Angriffs: Der Flugzeugträger"

So lautete der Angriffsbefehl, der durch den vernichtenden Bombentreffer, den Leutnant Francke auf einen englischen
Flugzeugträger am 26. .. 1939 erzielte, erfolgreich durchgeführt wurde

The German warship had six 11-inch guns and eight 5.9-inch guns. In weight of shell her armament completely outclassed the British force, the cruisers *Exeter*, *Ajax*, and *Achilles*, which between them only had six 8-inch guns (*Exeter*) and sixteen 6-inch guns (*Ajax* and *Achilles*). Moreover, *Graf Spee*'s heavier armour rendered her safe against anything but direct hits from *Exeter*'s 8-inch guns. Harwood, however, had already laid his plans for immediate action by day or night and he went straight into action, detaching *Exeter* to engage alone while he headed *Ajax* and *Achilles* to take the pocket-battleship in flank.

It took time for *Ajax* and *Achilles* to get into position—time enough for Langsdorff to concentrate the fire of his heavy guns on *Exeter* and make a floating wreck of her. All *Exeter*'s guns were knocked out; she was holed and flooding; but until the last possible minute her captain struggled to keep her in action, launching torpedoes, until *Exeter* was forced to drop out of the battle, trailing a dense pall of smoke, at about 0715 hours.

Ajax and *Achilles* continued the fight, trying to get close enough to do damage with their light guns, but soon *Ajax*, Harwood's flagship, came under *Graf Spee*'s 11-inch shellfire. Over half of *Ajax*'s guns were knocked out, and by now she had used up three-quarters of her ammunition. *Graf Spee*, however, seemed undamaged, and so *Ajax* and *Achilles* broke off the action at 0740 hours and retired out of range.

Captain Langsdorff had the game in his hands, but he could not see this. A humane and thoughtful commander, he was shaken by the losses to his crew: 36 killed and 59 wounded. The lighter British shells had caused no vital damage, but had inflicted enough superficial destruction to convince Langsdorff that *Graf Spee* could not tackle the wintry North Atlantic and the hazardous passage of the Denmark Strait. This was why he decided to run for Montevideo to seek time to make repairs first.

The Uruguayan authorities, however, urged by the British, granted Langsdorff only 72 hours' stay in Montevideo. This was in accordance with international law, for Uruguay was a neutral power; but it left Langsdorff with the choice of having his ship and his crew interned for the duration of the war, or putting to sea with his repairs far from completed. Moreover, he had accepted the many rumours in Montevideo (both natural and propaganda-inspired) that the British battle-cruiser *Renown* and the aircraft-carrier *Ark Royal* would be waiting for him when he came out. On December 17 he saw to it that *Graf Spee* was scuttled and sunk in the approaches to Montevideo harbour. Langsdorff could not bear to survive the loss of his ship: he shot himself on December 20, wrapped in the German ensign.

Allied co-operation at sea

The threat to the convoy routes caused by the appearance of the pocket-battleships in the Atlantic resulted in the setting-up of separate naval groups to hunt the raiders down. This in turn deepened the collaboration between the British and French navies. The French battle-cruisers *Dunkerque* and *Strasbourg* and three French 10,000-ton cruisers joined these

◁ △ *The* Gneisenau, *which formed, with her sister ship the* Scharnhorst, *the most powerful elements of the German fleet until the completion of the* Bismarck *and* Tirpitz.
◁ ▽ *Hitler and Grand-Admiral Raeder (*right foreground*). Hitler's ignorance of naval matters led him to give Raeder far more freedom in strategic and tactical matters than he was accustomed to give his generals.*
△ *French cruisers in line astern. The French Navy had several powerful and modern cruisers which proved a great boon when "hunting groups" had to be set up to deal with the German raiders.*

Antagonists at the Plate

The British heavy cruiser *Exeter*

Displacement: 8,390 tons. **Armament**: six 8-inch, four 4-inch A.A., and two 2-pounder A.A. guns, plus six 21-inch torpedo tubes, and two aircraft (as designed). **Armour**: 2- to 3-inch belt, $1\frac{1}{2}$- to 2-inch turrets, 2-inch deck, and 3-inch director tower. **Speed**: $32\frac{1}{2}$ knots. **Radius**: 10,000 miles at 14 knots. **Complement**: 630. **Length**: 575 feet. **Beam**: 58 feet. **Draught**: 20 feet 3 inches.

The German pocket-battleship *Admiral Graf Spee*

Displacement: 12,100 tons.
Armament: six 11-inch, eight 5.9-inch, six 4.1-inch A.A., eight 37-mm A.A., and ten 20-mm A.A. guns, plus eight 21-inch torpedo tubes, and two aircraft (as designed).
Armour: 4-inch belt, 2- to $5\frac{1}{2}$-inch turrets, $1\frac{1}{2}$- to 3-inch deck, and 2- to 5-inch control tower.
Speed: 26 knots. **Radius**: 19,000 miles at 19 knots.
Complement: 1,150. **Length**: 609 feet.
Beam: 70 feet. **Draught**: $21\frac{1}{2}$ feet.

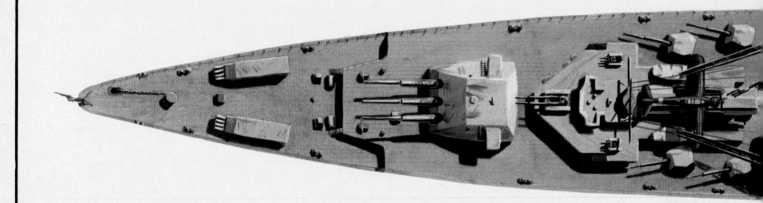

The British light cruiser *Ajax*

Displacement: 6,985 tons. **Armament**: eight 6-inch, eight 4-inch A.A., eight 2-pounder A.A., and twelve .5-inch guns, plus eight 21-inch torpedo tubes, and one aircraft (as designed). **Armour**: 2- to 4-inch belt, 1-inch turrets, 2-inch deck, and 1-inch director tower. **Speed**: 32½ knots. **Complement**: 550. **Length**: 554½ feet. **Beam**: 55¾ feet. **Draught**: 15½ feet.

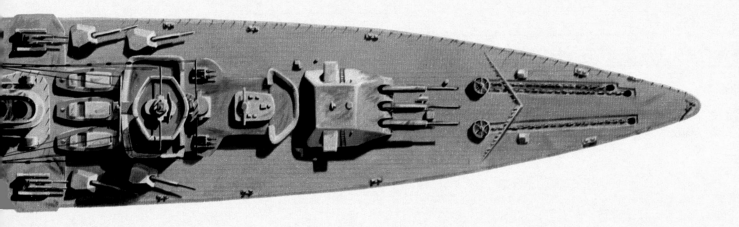

"hunting groups", as they were known and in the Indian Ocean the French cruiser *Suffren* was helping to guard the convoys bringing the first Australian troops to Egypt. On the British Admiralty's request, the dockyard workers in France were speeding up the completion of the new battleships *Richelieu* and *Jean Bart*, because of setbacks which were likely to delay the commissioning of their British counterparts, *King George V* and *Prince of Wales*.

As First Lord of the Admiralty, Churchill was keenly aware of the value of the Franco-British co-operation at sea. On the state of the French Navy he wrote: "the powerful fleet of France, which by the remarkable capacity and long administration of Admiral Darlan had been brought to the highest strength and degree of efficiency ever attained by the French Navy since the days of the Monarchy."

▷ *"Remember! Women and children first!"* Hitler orders his macabre crew as they prepare to open fire on the survivors of the Athenia. The Germans had tried to hush up the fact that one of their U-boats had sunk the unarmed liner on the first day of war; but the Allies were quick to exploit this example of "German atrocity", as this British propaganda cartoon indicates.
▽ *A Type IIB U-boat, one of the 30 small coastal boats that Germany used for training and on operations in the North Sea and the English Channel.*
▷ *Part of a German destroyer flotilla at sea.*

New menace: the magnetic mine

Another deadly weapon turned against the Anglo-French sea-lanes by Admiral Raeder was the magnetic mine. For the first months of the war at sea these mines did much damage and were a most serious worry to the Allies. Dropped from aircraft or laid by U-boat, the magnetic mine was detonated by the metallic mass of a ship passing over it. Such a submarine explosion from directly underneath usually resulted in the total destruction of the ship. Between November and December 1939, 59 Allied and neutral ships totalling 203,513 tons were sunk by magnetic mines.

But on the night of November 22–23 a German aircraft dropped a magnetic mine off Shoeburyness in the Thames Estuary. This landed on a mud-flat and was discovered at low tide. Commander J. G. D. Ouvry gallantly undertook to defuse the mine. It was a heroic piece of work: Ouvry went about his task, connected to the shore by a throat microphone into which he calmly described what he was about to do next. This was standard practice: if an accident or miscalculation had blown him to eternity, the next man to attempt to disarm a similar mine would at least know what not to attempt.

Ouvry succeeded, and the magnetic mine gave up its secrets. Once these were

1

2

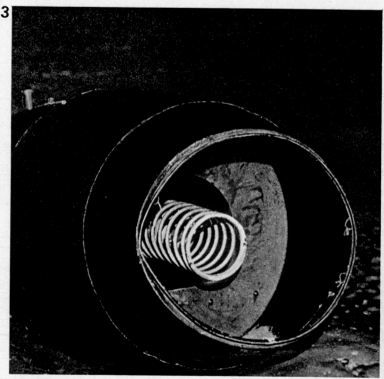

3

THE DEFEAT OF THE MAGNETIC MINE

1. The German magnetic mine as it appeared on the morning of November 23, 1939 just before Lieutenant-Commander Ouvry and Chief Petty Officer Baldwin set about defusing it. The ropes had been attached by the Army to stop the mine moving in the pre-dawn tide. This later proved to have been unnecessary, as the prongs on the right of the mine were designed to stop it moving.
2. The defused mine ready to be shipped off to H.M.S. Vernon, *the shore station in Portsmouth specialising in mines and torpedoes. There the mine was taken apart and the exact details of its mechanism worked out. It was discovered that the mine was detonated by the establishment of an electrical contact when the magnetic field of a ship deflected a balanced needle to complete the firing circuit.* 3. The rear of the mine, showing the powerful bronze spring that ejected the parachute to lower the weapon to the surface, after it was dropped by the mine-laying aircraft.
4. The bogey of the magnetic mine, manipulated by Hitler. This weapon was indeed a considerable threat, whose effects could have been disastrous for the Allied cause but for the swift solution of the problem by the British. 5. One of the answers to the magnetic mine: a Wellington fitted with a dural hoop, which produced a strong magnetic field when energised. If it flew over any such mine, the Wellington would detonate it,

leaving that portion of sea safe for shipping. 6. Another answer: "degaussing". In this, a metal belt run round the ship could be energised in such a way as to neutralise the ship's magnetic field, and thus prevent it from detonating any mine that the vessel might pass over.
7. Lieutenant-Commander Ouvry receives the D.S.O. from King George VI. The other members of the team were also decorated.

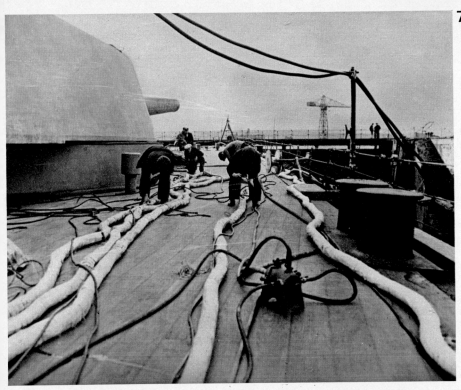

Rear-Admiral Karl Dönitz, commander of Germany's U-boats, was born in Grünau, near Berlin, on September 16, 1891. He joined the Navy in 1910, reaching the rank of Rear-Admiral on October 1, 1939. He was made Vice-Admiral in 1940, Admiral in 1942, and Grand-Admiral on January 30, 1943, when he was appointed Commander-in-Chief of the German Navy. He suceeded Hitler as Führer for 23 days in 1945 and was sentenced to goal by the Nuremberg Tribunal. He was released in 1956.

Lieutenant-Commander Günther Prien, victor over the *Royal Oak*, was born in 1908, and joined the German Merchant Navy in 1923 in the post-World War I depression. He started under sail, and obtained his Captain's ticket in 1932. But finding himself out of work he joined the Nazi Party and was with the labour corps before joining the Navy in 1933. He was posted to U-boats as soon as he had finished his basic training. Prien was lost with his ship in the Atlantic in March 1941.

known, ships began to be "degaussed" as a protective measure. Degaussing involved running a cable around the ship and passing an electric current throught it, which neutralised the ship's magnetic field. Degaussing operations on Allied ships had been largely completed by March 1940.

At the outbreak of war on September 3, Great Britain and France depended for their imports on a combined merchant fleet of 24 million tons. By the end of the year their total losses were well within the safety limit – and the magnetic mine had just been beaten. The Allied losses, moreover, were compensated for to a considerable degree by the amount of German merchant shipping captured or sunk: 75,000 tons.

Loss of the *Royal Oak*

The numerical odds were too far against the German Navy for there to be any thought of a deliberate engagement with the Allied fleets. Raeder could only wage a guerrilla war – but his U-boats and mine-layers did succeed in drawing blood at the Royal Navy's expense.

Two weeks after Britain had gone to war, on September 17, *U-29* (Lieutenant-Commander Otto Schuhart) sank the first Allied warship to be lost to enemy action in World War II: the elderly aircraft-carrier *Courageous* of 22,500 tons, which was lost with 519 of her crew.

Worse was to come. On the night of October 13–14, under a brilliant display of Northern Lights, Lieutenant-Commander Günther Prien took *U-47* through the maze of channels and currents girdling the stronghold of the British Home Fleet: the vast anchorage of Scapa Flow in the Orkneys, hitherto considered impenetrable to submarines. Prien found that the dog-leg channel in Holm Sound was more weakly defended than the others. He fired three torpedoes at the battleship *Royal Oak* (29,500 tons), which capsized and sank in 13 minutes, taking with her Rear-Admiral H. F. C. Blagrove and 832 crew.

The loss of this veteran warship of World War I made little or no difference to the Allies' superiority at sea, but the moral effect was enormous, both in Germany and Great Britain. Prien and his crew were welcomed as heroes in Berlin, and Prien himself was decorated with the Knight's Cross by Hitler. In London, there were wild rumours that the U-boat could only have got into Scapa Flow by treason, and for a while suspicion centred on a Swiss watchmaker in Kirkwall, largest town in the Orkneys. Not until the war was over was it proved for certain that the Scapa Flow feat had been carefully planned from Luftwaffe aerial reconnaissance photographs.

By mid-November the numerous French and British warships in the Atlantic, hunting what they believed to be two pocket-battleships, led Raeder to order a battle squadron to sail for the North Atlantic on November 21. It was hoped that a demonstration of force in the waters between Scotland and Iceland would draw off some Allied warships from the South Atlantic, easing the problems of *Graf Spee* (still at large). On November 23, the battle-cruisers *Scharnhorst* and *Gneisenau* surprised and obliterated the puny armed merchantman *Rawalpindi* west of the Faeroes.

Admiral Sir Charles Forbes, commanding the Home Fleet, was unable to put to sea and intercept these new raiders. On September 9, he had had to shift his base from Scapa Flow until the defences there – anti-aircraft as well as anti-submarine – had been put to rights. The new anchorages (at Loch Ewe on Scotland's west coast and at Rosyth in the Firth of Forth) were too far to the south to allow sufficient time to intercept German raiders in latitudes so far to the north. The Germans soon got wind of the Home Fleet's change of base and laid magnetic mines in the approaches to Loch Ewe; on December 4, one of them did so much damage to the battleship *Nelson* that she was out of action for several months.

Despite these setbacks, however, the Royal Navy, with the invaluable help of its French ally had, by the end of 1939, apparently achieved its double mission: to safeguard the sea-lanes of the Western Allies, and to cut those belonging to the common enemy. But this satisfactory situation was illusory. The German U-boat fleet was receiving new units at an alarming rate, and in any event was certainly not operating at full stretch. Despite the rapid elimination of *Graf Spee*, there was absolutely no guarantee that the Allies could prevent further surface raiders from reaching the Atlantic. And the problem of Germany's inshore supply-routes – those which ran through the territorial waters of Europe's neutral powers – had yet to be tackled.

◁ ▽ *Germany's first U-boat ace of the war, Günther Prien (in the white cap), together with his crew, was given a hero's welcome on his return from sinking the* Royal Oak *in Scapa Flow. He was fêted all the way to Berlin, and then had a triumphant reception in his country's capital.* ▽ *Propaganda for the armed forces. One of the headlines reports a British cruiser as sunk, but the only such vessel involved was the* Southampton, *on October 16 in the Firth of Forth. A 1,000-lb bomb had hit her amidships but failed to detonate.*

The German *U-47*

Displacement: 753/857 tons (surface/submerged).
Armament: five 21-inch torpedo tubes (four bow, one stern) with 15 torpedoes, or 14 mines, plus one 3.5-inch gun and one 20-mm A.A. gun.
Speed: $17\frac{1}{4}$/8 knots. **Radius:** 6,500 miles at 12 knots/80 miles at 4 knots.
Length: 218 feet. **Beam:** 20 feet 3 inches.
Draught: 15 feet 6 inches. **Complement:** 44.

The British *Royal Oak*

Displacement: 29,150 tons.
Armament: eight 15-inch, twelve 6-inch, eight 4-inch A.A., and sixteen 2-pounder A.A. guns, plus four 21-inch torpedo tubes and one aircraft.
Armour: 4- to 13-inch belt, 1- to $5\frac{1}{2}$-inch deck, $4\frac{1}{4}$- to 13-inch turrets, and 11- to 13-inch conning tower.
Speed: $21\frac{1}{2}$ knots.
Length: 620 feet 6 inches.
Beam: 102 feet 6 inches.
Draught: 28 feet 6 inches.
Complement: 1,146.

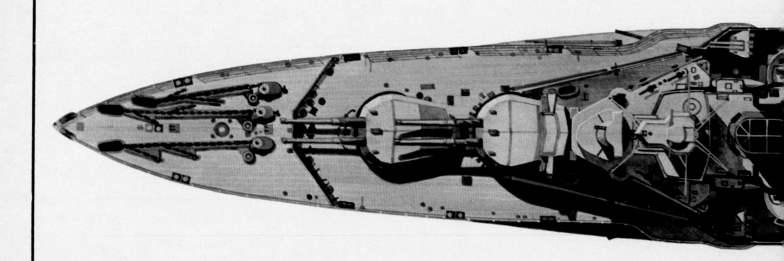

The Sinking of the *Royal Oak*

Hatston Naval Air Station

Kirkwall

Burra Sound

GRAEMSAY

Bring Deeps

Royal Oak Sunk 14·10·39

Scapa Flow

CAVA

Gutter Sound

LAMB HOLM

HOY

FARA

BURRAY

Destroyer Anchorage

Naval Base

FLOTTA

Hoxa Sound

HMS Iron Duke

Long Hope

Switha Sound

SOUTH RONALDSAY

SWONA

→ ROUTE TAKEN IN & OUT OF
⇢ SCAPA FLOW BY U-47
— BOOM DEFENCES
-- BLOCKSHIPS
— GUARD & MINE LOOPS
-- INDICATOR LOOPS
▨ ANTI-U-BOAT NETS

0 MILES   5

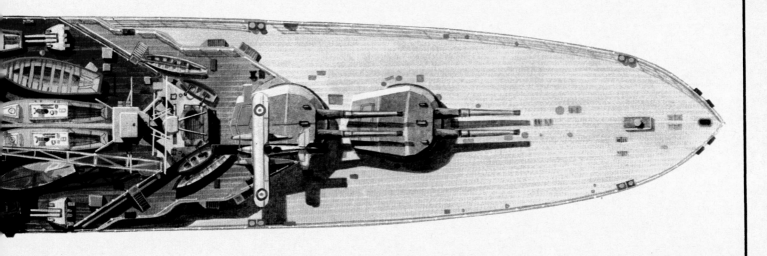

CHAPTER 11
Finland: the winter war

After the German-Soviet Treaty of September 28, 1939, the Soviet Government imposed "mutual defence agreements" upon Estonia, Latvia, and Lithuania. These provide for the garrisoning of Soviet troops on the islands of Dagö and Osel in Estonia, and at Windau and Libau in Latvia.

Moscow then proceeded to make similar demands upon Finland. On October 14, a Finnish delegation in Moscow listened to the following claims, put to them by Stalin, Molotov, and Deputy Foreign Commissar Potemkin:

1. Finland to cede her islands in the Gulf of Finland;
2. Finland to withdraw her frontier in the Karelian Isthmus between the Baltic and Lake Ladoga;
3. An aero-naval base at Hangö at the mouth of the Gulf of Finland to be leased by Finland to the Soviet Union for 30 years;
4. Finland to cede to the Soviet Union her portion of the Rybachiy Peninsula in Lappland; and
5. Conclusion of a mutual assistance treaty, between the Soviet Union and Finland, for the defence of the Gulf of Finland.

In compensation for these sacrifices, Moscow offered Finland an "adjustment" (albeit a considerable one) of the frontier in Karelia.

Faced with these demands, the Finnish Government of President Cajander did not reject the proposals outright. After consultation with Marshal Carl Gustav Mannerheim, Commander-in-Chief of Finland's armed forces, the Finnish Government inclined towards compromise as far as the islands in the gulf and the Karelian frontier were concerned, provided only that the fortified line across the isthmus remained in Finnish hands; but all claims for the base at Hangö and for the frontier adjustments in the Rybachiy Peninsula were rejected.

Deadlock was reached on October 23, when the Russians refused to budge an inch from their proposals of the 14th and the Finns, led by Ministers Paasikivi and Tanner, held equally firmly to their counter-proposals. After a month of fruitless discussion, Molotov announced on November 26 that Finnish artillery had opened fire on Soviet troops, and demanded that the Finnish troops should retire 15 miles from the frontier. The Helsinki Government did not reject the demand: it simply asked that as a condition for such a retirement, Soviet Russia should withdraw her troops the same distance on her side of the frontier. This tipped the scale, and on November 30 the Soviet land, sea, and air forces took the offensive against Finland without any declaration of war.

David and Goliath

The Soviet official *History of the Great Patriotic War* contains no information of any use concerning the opening phase of

▽ *Finnish infantryman in winter clothing. Gliding through their native forests as no Russian troops could, these élite Finnish marksmen were a constant thorn in the sides of more ponderous Soviet units.*

The Gloster Gladiator I

Engine: one Bristol Mercury IX radial, 830-hp at 14,500 feet.
Armament: two .303-inch Browning machine guns in the fuselage with 600 rounds per gun, and two .303-inch Browning machine guns with 400 rounds per gun.
Speed: 253 mph at 14,500 feet. **Climb:** 4 minutes 40 seconds to 10,000 feet. **Ceiling:** 32,800 feet. **Range:** 428 miles.
Weight empty/loaded: 3,217/4,592 lbs. **Span:** 32 feet 3 inches.
Length: 27 feet 5 inches. **Height:** 11 feet 9 inches.
(This aircraft was British-built, owned by the Swedish Air Force, and flown by their 19th Squadron in Finnish markings in northern Finland during the early months of 1940.)

△ △ *Finland's struggle against Communism aroused the sympathy and admiration of the Western democracies. But though money was raised, and limited quantities of armaments were sent, Finland did not receive what she needed more desperately – trained and fully-equipped fighting men to supplement the trickle of Scandinavian volunteers.* △ *"It's only the same old steamroller." But though the Western powers could laugh at the inefficiency and inertia of the Russian war machine in 1940, they were to be only too pleased to have it on their side from 1941 onwards*

the "Winter War" – no orders of battle, names of generals, or any of the normal statistics usually quoted in abundance by Soviet historians. But on November 30, 1939, it can be estimated that the Red Army deployed against Finland 19 rifle (infantry) divisions and five tank brigades, grouped into the following armies:

1. Karelian Isthmus: 7th Army, with eight divisions, a tank corps, and two independent tank brigades, was to force the defences of the Mannerheim Line, take Viipuri, and push on to Helsinki by the third day of the offensive;
2. East shore of Lake Ladoga: 8th Army, with six divisions, was to assist 7th Army in its frontal attack by drawing off the Finnish defence;
3. Central Finland: 9th Army, with four divisions, was to launch two columns across the "waist" of Finland, the left column making for Oulu and the right for Kemi; and
4. Lappland: 14th Army, with one division, was to take Petsamo and sever northern Finland's communications with Norway.

Because of the growing tension between Finland and the Soviet Union, the Helsinki Government had already proceeded to call up the Finnish reserves; but on the day of the Soviet attack, Marshal Mannerheim had only nine divisions at his disposal:

1. Karelian Isthmus: five divisions (II and III Corps) under the command of Lieutenant-General Hugo Ostermann;
2. East shore of Lake Ladoga: two divisions (IV Corps) under Major-General Hägglund;
3. Central Finland: a screen of nine frontier battalions (V Corps) under Major-General Vilpo Tuompo;
4. Lappland: four independent battalions under Major-General Kurt Wallenius; and
5. In reserve: two incomplete divisions (I Corps) and a cavalry brigade.

Finland's full mobilisation would provide the manpower for 15 divisions, but she faced the initial onslaught with only 120,000 Finnish against 300,000 Soviet troops, well-armed and backed up by 800 aircraft. Finland's air force had about 100 aircraft, and many of these were not battle-worthy.

The Finnish soldiers – used to the forest, efficient hunters, skilled on skis, and natural fighters – soon showed themselves to be master-practioners of the art of irregular warfare. True, their weapons

were neither modern nor fully adequate. The Finnish *Suomi* 9-mm submachine gun functioned perfectly in sub-zero conditions, but it was not a weapon ideally suited to forest warfare. Nor were the improvised incendiary grenades known as "Molotov cocktails". The Finnish Army also contained 90,000 female auxiliaries (known as *Lottas*) – a telling commentary on the patriotism of Finland's small population of 3,700,000.

Two circumstances favoured the defenders. First was the terrain. Finland's vast forests gave ample cover and allowed the small detachments in which the Finnish Army operated to launch ambushes on the few roads that penetrated their forests. Second was the winter cold; this froze up the 35,000 lakes which would otherwise have helped the defenders even more, but the abnormal temperatures of the winter of 1939–40 (often 30 or 40 degrees below zero on the Centigrade scale) hit the Russians far harder than the Finns, for the latter were falling back on their own strongpoints and were able to make more effective use of a "scorched earth" policy in so doing.

None of this, however, would have been of value without the admirable resolve of the Finnish nation, which ignored the blandishments of the Communist leader Otto Kuusinen and his "People's Government of the Finnish Democratic Republic", set up at Terijoki behind the Soviet lines. The Finns disowned him virtually to a man; and Kuusinen soon became so great an embarrassment to the Soviet Government, in view of the disastrous failures of the Red Army in the field, that he was quietly abandoned in the early part of 1940.

Fiasco time for the Red Army

By the end of 1939 the Red Army had suffered a series of resounding and humiliating defeats.

In the Karelian Isthmus, advancing on a front of 87 miles, the Soviet 7th Army was stopped in its tracks by the Mannerheim Line's pillboxes and anti-tank obstacles. The Soviet 8th Army, advancing in support of the 7th on the far shore of Lake Ladoga, suffered even worse: after its 139th and 75th Divisions reached Tolvajärvi on December 12, they were

ambushed and cut to pieces by seven Finnish battalions under Colonel Talvela, in an action which cost the Russians over 5,000 dead.

In central Finland, the Soviet column from 9th Army advancing on Oulu was counter-attacked at Suomussalmi by Colonel Siilasvuo's detachment. On December 11, the Soviet 163rd Division was cut off; on the 28th, the Soviet 44th Division, trying to retreat, was ambushed and destroyed in turn.

Accurate figures of Russian losses are not available, but the Red Army lost about 27,500 dead against a total figure of 2,700 Finnish dead and wounded. The Finns also captured 80 tanks and 70 guns, and rounded up 1,600 prisoners-of-war.

The fact that so few prisoners were taken proves that the Russian soldier knew how to fight and die. This is not the impression given by the Soviet *History of the Great Patriotic War*, which tends to blame the troops. A typical critical passage reads: "In attack the Soviet troops showed certain failures in preparation and command. Some formations had been insufficiently trained in fighting on skis, in sub-zero conditions, and in regions of dense forests and lakes. There was lack of experience in attacking permanent installations and concrete emplacements."

Stalin and Molotov were to a great extent to blame for having made light of the patriotism of the Finnish people, and so were their military advisers for having misjudged the capacity for resistance and the manoeuvrability displayed by the Finnish Army. In addition to this, grave blunders had been made by the Soviet High Command, most notably the suicidal tactic of sending armoured and motorised columns along forest roads where there was no possibility of manoeuvre.

Throughout the campaign, Hitler maintained a malevolent neutrality towards Finland. To the great indignation of Ciano, he forbade the transit across Germany of Italian war material intended for Finland.

△ *A scene typical of the Winter War. Time and time again, Russian columns were caught on narrow forest roads and annihilated by the more mobile and enterprising Finns. But the Russians learnt quickly—and the next stage of the war was to be altogether different.*

The Russian BT-7-2

Weight: 13.8 tons.
Crew: three.
Armament: one 45-mm gun with 188 rounds and two 7.62-mm machine guns with 2,394 rounds.
Armour: hull front 22-mm; turret front, sides, and rear 15-mm; hull sides and rear 13-mm; turret roof 10-mm; and hull floor and roof 6- to 10-mm.
Engine: M-17T 12-cylinder V inline, 450-hp.
Speed: $45\frac{1}{2}$ mph on its road wheels (with the tracks removed) and 33 mph on its tracks.
Range: 310 miles on wheels; 220 miles on tracks.
Length: 18 feet $7\frac{3}{4}$ inches.
Width: 8 feet.
Height: 7 feet 6 inches.

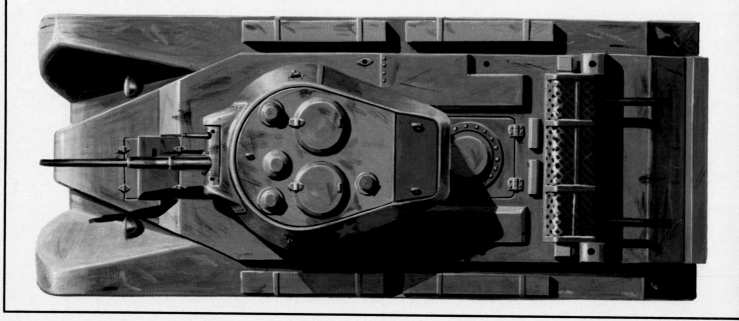